About Demos

Demos is a greenhouse for new ideas which can improve the quality of our lives. As an independent think tank, we aim to create an open resource of knowledge and learning that operates beyond traditional party politics.

We connect researchers, thinkers and practitioners to an international network of people changing politics. Our ideas regularly influence government policy, but we also work with companies, NGOs, colleges and professional bodies.

Demos knowledge is organised around five themes, which combine to create new perspectives. The themes are democracy, learning, enterprise, quality of life and global change.

But we also understand that thinking by itself is not enough. Demos has helped to initiate a number of practical projects which are delivering real social benefit through the redesign of public services.

We bring together people from a wide range of backgrounds to cross-fertilise ideas and experience. By working with Demos, our partners develop a sharper insight into the way ideas shape society. For Demos, the process is as important as the final product.

www.demos.co.uk

First published in 2003

ISBN 1 84180 107 0
Typeset by Land & Unwin, Bugbrooke
Printed by Printflow, London

For further information and
subscription details please contact:

Demos
The Mezzanine
Elizabeth House
39 York Road
London SE1 7NQ

telephone: 020 7401 5330
email: mail@demos.co.uk
web: www.demos.co.uk

The New Old

Why baby boomers won't be pensioned off

Julia Huber and
Paul Skidmore

DEMOS

Contents

Acknowledgements

We are very grateful to Age Concern for supporting this project and particularly thank Neil Churchill for his contribution throughout the research process. Thanks also to Stephanie Harlan, James Bridge and Yvonne Reid.

Special thanks are owed to MORI, and Jane Robinson, Roger Mortimore and Simon Atkinson in particular, for providing us with survey data and helping us with the analysis.

We are indebted to many experts for their comments and advice on the ideas in this pamphlet and particularly thank John Rother and Dr Sara Rix from the AARP. Thanks also to Professor Roger Jowell, Michael Willmott, Paul Wallace, Professor Alan Walker, Marg Walker, Leon Kreitzman, Susan Hewer, Frank Field and Ben Forsyth, Maria Evandrou, Andrew Cracknell, Don Steele, Paul Burstow and Richard Stokoe, Helen Bray, Maggie Semple, Penny Cooper, Professor Tony Warnes, Laurie South, Dr David Metz, Huguette Boyagis, Tom Cairns, Adriana Falger, Dr Maria Theofilatou, Sally Greengross and Mark McLaren, and Simon Sylvester. We would also like to thank Adele Blakebrough, Ann Kramer, Valerie Thomas, Adam Hart and John Holden for sharing some of their experiences, and everyone who participated in the Demos/Age Concern seminar series on baby boomers.

We would like to thank our colleagues at Demos past and present for their support, and especially Rachel Jupp for getting the project up and running. Thanks also to Eddie Gibb, Peter Macleod, James Wilsdon and James Harkin. Finally, our thanks to Tom Bentley for his guidance and inspiration when it was most needed.

All of these people and many more made invaluable contributions; any omissions or errors remain our own.

Julia Huber
Paul Skidmore
July 2003

1. Welcome to the ageing society

Turn a pyramid upside down and it falls over.
Paul Wallace, *Agequake*

You can never plan the future by the past.
Edmund Burke[1]

Demographers and economists have run the numbers and they don't look good. Over the next 50 years the age pyramid of the population will be turned upside down. The 2001 census revealed that people aged 60 and over already outnumber children under-16 in the UK for the first time.[2] In 2040, there will be 5 million more people aged over 65 than there were at the turn of the millennium.[3]

An ageing population has long been conceived as a burden and a cost, as if the old were some kind of tax on the young. We have grown accustomed to hearing about the demographic 'time bomb', a phrase that captures the sense of threat which an ageing society is seen to present, particularly in terms of the sustainability of key public policies like pensions, health and long-term care. But there is a cardinal error in projecting today's expectations and assumptions onto tomorrow's numbers. The result is a public debate that is highly negative, focused almost exclusively on the economic and fiscal dimensions of an ageing society at the expense of its wider, and deeper, social, cultural and political implications.

Being literate in the language of demographic change does not by itself improve our clairvoyance about the kind of society that it will help to shape. Demographic tools may allow us to predict how the age structure of populations will change over time. But while the trends themselves are broadly predictable, the way in which society – its institutions, cultural norms and values – will adapt (or not) to accommodate such a transition is much less clear. In the first place, as a strand of recent Demos work has shown, complex social systems like these tend to respond to change in unpredictable and non-linear ways.[4] Second, demographic change must be understood as taking place in a context that is inherently dynamic, yet our predictions about the impact of an ageing society are often very static. It is as though we are trying to drive looking only in the rear view mirror, interpreting the world through the lens of what has passed before not what lies ahead. The salient features of contemporary society will not remain in suspended animation over the coming decades, but will instead be subject to an array of potentially disruptive forces, including:

- declining confidence and trust in politics and public institutions
- the impact and handling of new technologies
- quality of life and the quest for more sustainable models of economic growth
- growing social diversity
- the relationship between OECD countries and people in the developing world.

The response to these challenges will transform the everyday routines and operating procedures of social and institutional life, making it impossible to isolate the impact of any one set of variables on the overall capacity for adaptation to and accommodation of change. The transition to an ageing society, in short, will be inextricably bound up in the way these issues play out, and very difficult to predict in advance.

But the biggest unknown in all of this is tomorrow's older generation itself – the 'new old' – and what it thinks and feels about the transition it is facing. At every stage of their lives, the baby boomers have been at the forefront of radical social, economic and political change: within the family, within the education system, within the labour market, and beyond. The way that members of this age group, the most influential generation in recent social history, choose to adapt to their changing circumstances will have a similarly dramatic impact in their later life.

The political challenge is therefore not simply determining the policy priorities needed to navigate the coming transition, but whether we can build the necessary institutions, social expectations and political legitimacy in time to influence its outcome. And for that to happen the key players need to start now.

It is true that Britain is relatively well prepared for the transition compared with many other countries. Despite widespread concern about the existence of a 'pensions time-bomb', for example, public pension spending as a percentage of GDP in the UK is currently around 5 per cent and is projected to remain at a similar level over the next half century.[5] Ageing has also been identified as a new priority across a range of policy areas, from community cohesion to employment discrimination. However, despite the emphasis on ageing within specific policy domains there is little indication of a coherent, overarching strategy. Unlike many of its counterparts the UK government has yet to set out a clear policy vision for the third age. Meanwhile, gaping holes in our social and economic provision remain and, far from being filled by the current emphasis on 'voluntaristic' approaches, they are becoming more stark.

But more importantly, on a whole series of key issues confronting society we do not know which way the baby boomers will jump, or if they will all jump together. These issues include:

- their wealth and living standards versus wider questions of social or intergenerational equity, and what this means for the renegotiation of the historic welfare compact

- their definition of quality of life in terms of lifestyle, economic participation and public and community goods (such as public services)
- their attitude to political engagement, their readiness to identify or act as a group and their potentially crucial electoral impact as a 'swing' constituency of voters.

It is the combination of these issues, the lines along which they serve to segment the baby boom cohort, that is most crucial.

What has been missing from the ageing debate so far (at least in the UK) is any serious interrogation of the values and attitudes that the baby boomers will bring to the table. The question of whether this generation will be willing to enrol in the progressive transformation of our society, or whether it just wants to be left alone to enjoy its retirement, will fundamentally determine the collective outcomes of societal ageing. Yet, for now, this is a question that we seem curiously ill-equipped to answer.

This report is an initial attempt to bring together what we do know, and to map it against some of the key challenges that an ageing society presents. In this sense, it is designed to be agenda-setting rather than definitive, and to act as a platform for further, more exhaustive research and enquiry. It has been written against the backdrop of widespread political attention on a few narrow dimensions of ageing. But so far this debate has generated more heat than light, and has failed to move the argument beyond the impasse that long-term policy challenges, coupled with short-term political imperatives, have created.

We should proceed from the recognition that this transition – and the choices it presents us with – will be resolved one way or the other. The question is whether it will happen in a last-minute and fragmented way, or whether it can be a positive experience for the whole of society. If it is to be the latter, then we must abandon a policy agenda skewed towards 'damage limitation', aimed simply at re-creating *post*-transition society in its *pre*-transition image while minimising the transaction costs of doing so. Instead we should begin to focus on the kind of positive life goals for older people that could become 'poles of attraction' around which a whole range of individual and collective choices can begin to cohere. Rather than locking the issues into a narrow debate about social security, and risk encouraging future generations of older people simply to unite around defending what they perceive as their entitlements, we need to imagine the principles on which a range of fully fledged alternative social, economic and cultural arrangements might be based. More specifically, we believe the following principles should be placed at the heart of the political agenda:

- social equity
- sustainability
- quality of life.

The report examines who the members of the baby boomer generation are, what we know about their values and attitudes, and how the key challenges of economic and community participation, self-fulfilment, quality of life, and family and intergenerational obligation might be met through a more positive and proactive approach to the issues and the potential for innovation. In addressing these questions we also examine current policies and conventional wisdom, and examples of new approaches and solutions that could play a bigger part in the future.

We conclude this chapter with 11 challenges that could form part of a positive agenda for all sectors to make society a better place to be old, and in turn to increase the contribution that the 'new old' can make to the quality of everybody else's lives.

Challenge 1
Harness 'elderpreneurship' by creating new models of economic participation that allow older people to use their skills and assets creatively for longer.

Challenge 2
Remodel local life through the physical redesign of neighbourhoods

and housing stock to maximise the integration and independence of older people in wider and more diverse communities.

Challenge 3
Create opportunities for civic participation and leadership that explicitly draw on the time and experience of older people, and widen the range of public representation. In the process, we need to re-create and validate a twenty-first-century notion of the 'community elder'.

Challenge 4
Build new forms of mutual and public support around the 'beanpole' family, and redefine the rights and responsibilities of family life to maximise the value of intergenerational transfer in both directions, while making the needs of young children a central focus for all generations.

Challenge 5
Develop policies that not only prevent extreme pensioner poverty but also help prevent a significant minority of older people being pushed into continued 'service-class' employment because of economic insecurity.

Challenge 6
Develop a sustainable market for social care that is intertwined with a robust, realistic emphasis on 'communities of care'.

Challenge 7
Capitalise on the baby boomers' insatiable appetite for learning by providing new forms of access and entitlement to knowledge and culture, and building new organisations capable of identifying, matching and refreshing labour market skills.

Challenge 8
Create workplace cultures that place as much emphasis on 'succession' and transfer of experience as they do on 'recruitment'.

Challenge 9
Develop a communications culture that is more effective at reaching, engaging and building trust by appealing to the growing desire to 'age well' and be treated as a mature consumer or citizen rather than catering to short-term appetites or targeting the assumption that the purpose of life is to perpetuate youth.

Challenge 10
Develop an approach to public service delivery that makes active participation in social networks and health-giving activities equal in status to the dispensation of standardised expert services.

Challenge 11
Stimulate a new public debate about the 'legacies' passed from one generation to another and the responsibilities of older generations towards the future, and the nature of a 'good death'.

To sum up:

- The implications of the ageing society will be profound, but they cannot readily be predicted on the basis of abstract demographic trends.
- These outcomes will be made real by the collective and individual choices we make about how best to adapt to an ageing society.
- The problem is that our assumptions about the future are rooted in a particular conception of older generations, but the baby boomers have transformed every station they have passed through and show no sign of stopping in old age. As a result, we must confront the conceptual framework we use to think about ageing and the conventional wisdom about the central political or governance challenge it poses.
- Conceptually, we need to focus less on abstract demographic or economic trends and look in much closer detail at the

underlying social, cultural and attitudinal characteristics of the baby boomer generation.

- Politically, we need to stop trying to limit the damage demographic change will do to current systems and structures, and start creating the conditions for a dialogue from which whole new ones can emerge.

2. The world in 2050

Throughout the twentieth century declining fertility and increasing longevity have been steadily transforming the demographic profile of populations across the world. The estimates of how it is going to change in the first half of this century make disturbing reading.[6] Let us begin by taking a brief journey to see what the world in 2050 looks like:

- *In 2050, there are 2 billion people in the world aged 60 or over* This is more than triple the number of people in the world 50 years earlier at the turn of the millennium; the number then was 600 million, which was in turn triple the figure in 1950.
- *One in three people in the developed world is aged over 60, as is one in five in less-developed regions* Fifty years earlier the figure was 20 per cent (one in five) in the developed world and just 8 per cent (around one in thirteen) in less-developed regions.
- *In Europe, there are 51 people aged 65 or over for every 100 aged 15 –64* This old-age dependency ratio has increased from 22 per 100 in the year 2000. It has also increased:
  - from 6 to 11 per 100 in Africa
  - from 9 to 26 per 100 in Asia, Latin America and the Caribbean
  - from 15 to 29 per 100 in Oceania

  - from 19 to 35 per 100 in North America.
- *In 2050, one-fifth of older people are 80 years old or older* This group, the 'oldest-old', constituted one-tenth of the total population of older persons in 2000, but they were also the fastest-growing age group in the world.
- *In 2050, the 'average' median age of the world's population is 36 years* Fifty years earlier, the median age was only 26 years.

The UK picture

As a developed country, the UK is at a relatively more advanced stage of the demographic transition than the less-developed countries. For example, in 2000 the 'average' median age in Britain was already 38.8 years. This will rise to 42.6 by 2025.[7]

Over the past 50 years the population of the UK has aged considerably. While the proportion aged under-16 has decreased from 24 per cent to 20 per cent, the population aged over 60 has increased from 16 per cent to 21 per cent.[8] This process will accelerate over the next decades. The number of people aged over 65 is projected to increase by more than 1 million to reach 11.9 million in 2011. By 2040, it will have risen to more than 15 million,[9] see figure 2.1.

As a result, the UK's old-age dependency ratio is also set to grow rapidly. In 1975 there were just over 22 people aged 65 and over per 100 people aged 15–64. By 2000, this had only increased to a little over 24 per 100, but is now set to rise quickly to nearly 35 per 100 in 2025, and to 47 per 100 in 2050.[10]

In Britain, as elsewhere, it is the 'oldest-old' that as a group will swell most dramatically between 2000 and 2025. The number of people aged 80 and over will increase by almost half during this period, from 2.4 million in 2000 to 3.5 million in 2025. Longer-term projections suggest that the population of those aged 80 and over will then grow even more rapidly, to 4.9 million by 2040, more than double the number at the turn of the millennium.[11] Table 2.1 shows the changes in life expectancy at age 65 and figure 2.2 shows the projected population pyramid for the UK between 2001 and 2031.

Figure 2.1 Actual and projected population aged under 16 and over 65 in the UK, 1981–2041

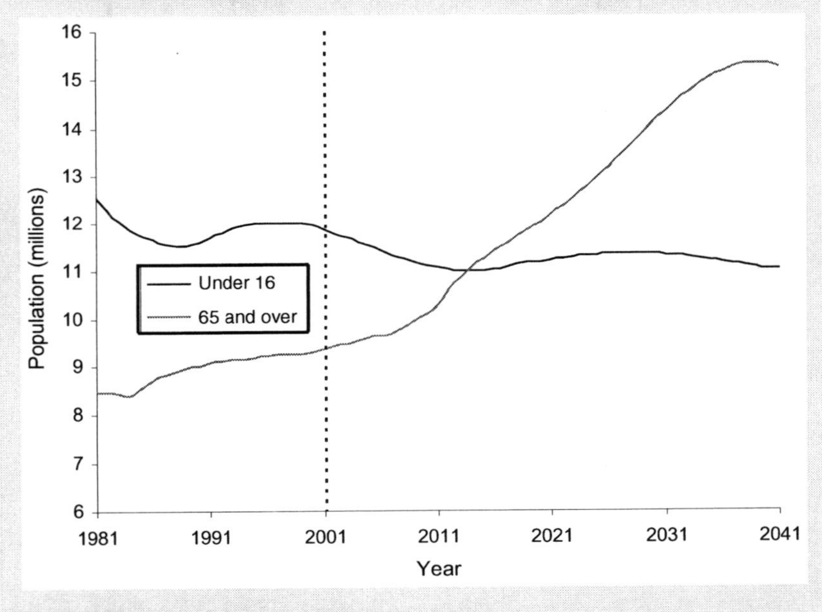

Source: Government Actuary's Department, 2003

Table 2.1 Changes in life expectancy at age 65

Year	Life expectancy at age 65 (yrs)	
	Men	Women
1928	11.5	13.3
1960	12.1	15.3
2002	16.0	19.0
2025	18.3	21.1
2050	19.0	21.7

Source: Government Actuary's Department, cited in: *Simplicity, Security and Choice: working and saving for retirement*, 2002

Figure 2.2 Population projection pyramid for the UK, 2001–2031

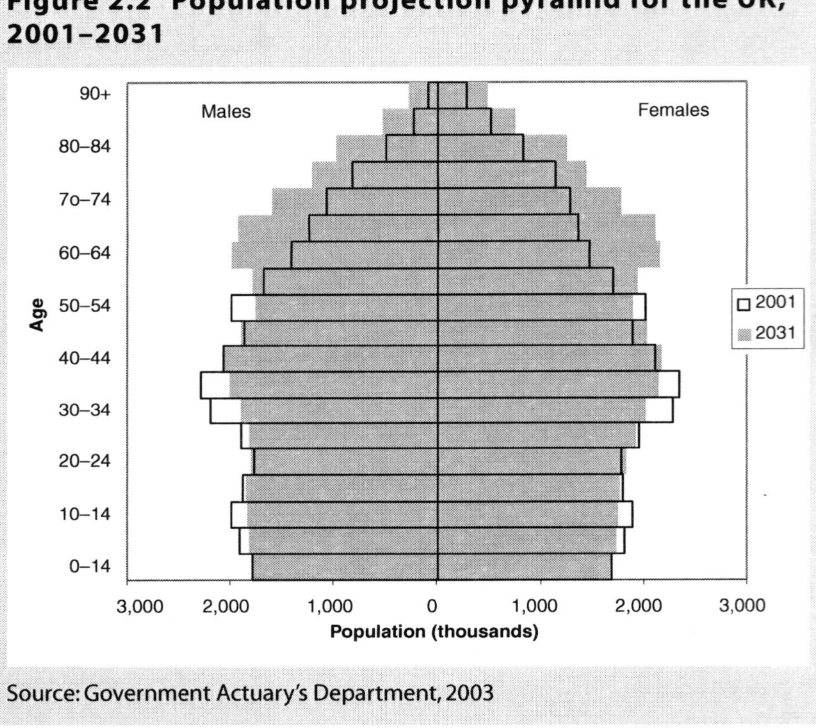

Source: Government Actuary's Department, 2003

The political response in the UK and abroad

Confronted with demographic change on this scale, policy-makers have tended to gravitate towards a highly negative interpretation of the implications of an ageing society. The World Bank's 1994 report *Averting the Old Age Crisis* is the expression *par excellence* of this kind of discourse, and the gloomy picture it evokes is worth quoting at length:

> Systems providing financial security for the old are under increasing *strain* throughout the world. Rapid demographic transitions caused by rising life expectancy and declining fertility mean that the proportion of old people in the general

> population is growing rapidly. Extended families and other traditional ways of supporting the old are *weakening*. Meanwhile, formal systems, such as government-backed pensions, have proved both *unsustainable* and very *difficult* to reform...The result is a *looming* old age *crisis* that *threatens* not only the old but also their children and grandchildren, who must *shoulder*, directly or indirectly, much of the increasingly heavy *burden* of providing for the aged [emphasis added].[12]

More specifically, the debate has centred on how to minimise the transaction costs of re-creating *post*-transition society in its *pre*-transition image. The policy agenda has come to resemble little more than a damage limitation exercise in those domains where an ageing society threatens to disrupt or undermine the stability of current arrangements. The most important of these are:

- pensions
- work and retirement
- health
- long-term care.

Pensions

It has become increasingly common to talk of the 'pensions crisis' facing developed countries, but for the sake of clarity it is helpful to distinguish between two crises: the first collective, the second individual.

First, public pensions have largely been organised on a 'pay-as-you-go' basis, where current tax receipts are used to fund current pensions. This makes them sensitive to changes in the number of pensioners needing to be supported by those in employment. The risk that this posed to the long-term health of the public finances was one of the reasons invoked by the Thatcher government for the radical switch in pension policy it engineered from the early 1980s. This combined:

- an erosion of the value of the basic state pension, through the severing of the link between average earnings and pension benefits
- an increase in the incentives to opt out of state provision and into tax-subsidised private pension schemes of various kinds
- a steady shift towards an increasingly 'voluntaristic' pensions policy, where the state provides only a limited safety net and places the onus on individuals to provide for their own security in retirement.

As a deliberate result of this voluntaristic approach, public pension spending as a percentage of GDP in the UK is currently around 5 per cent, and is projected to remain at a similar level over the next half century.[13] This is in marked contrast to many continental European countries, which face much greater public pension commitments.

Yet fears about the impact of an ageing society have not subsided and another 'crisis' has emerged. Concern about the potential collective risk to the Exchequer has given way to concerns about the risk to particular individuals of under-saving. The government's recent green paper *Simplicity, Security and Choice* acknowledged for the first time that in the future some individuals will suffer serious pension shortfalls if certain aspects of the current system are not improved:

> Current estimates show that up to 3 million people are seriously under-saving for their retirement – or planning to retire too soon. In addition, a further group of between 5 and 10 million people may want to consider saving more, working longer, or a combination of both, depending on their expectations for retirement.[14]

The Labour government has introduced a range of measures designed to tackle the 'savings gap', but these have sought to extend and improve the voluntaristic approach rather than transcend it.

Stakeholder pensions were introduced in 2001, designed to offer a simple, low-cost savings vehicle for people on lower incomes. They are widely seen to have failed to reach their target market and face mounting hostility from the insurance industry.[15] Two recent surveys by the Consumer Association found that 46 per cent of the UK workforce is not contributing to a pension scheme, and of these only 8 per cent are thinking about taking up a pension in the near future.[16] A new means-tested Pension Credit is being introduced in October 2003 to provide a minimum income for less well-off pensioners, while mitigating some of the disincentives to save that had existed previously under Income Support and the Minimum Income Guarantee. The green paper also proposed a number of initiatives to simplify the pensions framework for individuals and employers, to enable consumers to make better and more informed choices, and protect those already in pensions schemes.[17]

Work and retirement

One direct corollary of the perceived crisis in pensions provision has been a growing emphasis on increasing labour market participation among older age groups, and encouraging people to work beyond the current state pension age. In the UK and many other countries early retirement and low employment rates are particularly prevalent among those aged 50 and over. The average age of withdrawal from the labour force in the UK is 62.6, more than two years before the official state pension age.[18] Employment rates for men and women start to tail off steeply after age 55, and by age 65 around two-thirds of all men and half of all women have left the labour force.[19] A third of 50–65 year olds, almost 3 million people, are outside the labour market.[20] In policy terms, this emphasis manifested itself in four main ways.

Active labour market policy The government's flagship programme for helping those aged 50 and over to return to work is New Deal 50 Plus, an active labour market policy under the umbrella of the government's 'welfare-to-work' programme aimed specifically at people aged over 50 who are out of work and claiming benefit. The *Simplicity, Security and Choice* green paper sought to build and improve on this foundation by 'providing extra back-to-work help for those aged 50 and over and piloting measures to help recipients of incapacity benefits return to work'.[21]

Another important dimension of this has been the encouragement of life-long learning through continuous training and skill development, which has increasingly been seen as an essential part of enabling older workers to remain in work longer.[22]

Encouraging work beyond state pension age A central focus of *Simplicity, Security and Choice* was the need to increase the flexibility of the current state pension age and to encourage people to carry on working longer. Although the government stopped short of raising the state pension age, the green paper proposed a mix of carrots and sticks to make it more flexible. The carrots included:[23]

- amending tax and pension rules to ensure that they do not discourage flexible retirement, including making it possible for individuals to draw an occupational pension while continuing to work for the employer
- increasing the financial incentive to delay drawing a pension – from 2010 people will earn at least a 10 per cent increase (rather than the current 7.5 per cent increase) for each year they delay drawing their pension
- offering people who defer taking their pension a choice of either increased regular state pension or a taxable lump-sum payment, comparable to the value of the pension increase.

while the sticks included:[24]

- raising the earliest age from which a pension may be taken from age 50 to 55 by 2010
- treating men and women between 60 and 64 as active labour market participants.

Age discrimination Alongside these formal barriers to labour market entry, the government is also committed to tackling the informal obstacles and disincentives created by age discrimination. By December 2006 the government will implement the EU Employment Directive on Equal Treatment,[25] which will prohibit age discrimination in employment and vocational training. The directive will, for instance, make the setting of compulsory retirement ages by employers unlawful unless the employer can prove objectively that it would be justified.

The government has also launched the Age Positive campaign, which aims to change employers' attitudes towards older people and 'help employers recognise the business benefits of an age-diverse workforce'. At the heart of the campaign is the Code of Practice on Age Diversity in Employment, which encourages employers not to make decisions that discriminate by age.[26]

Most recently, the government published *Equality and Diversity: Age matters*, its consultation on proposals for age discrimination legislation in line with the EU Employment Directive. The proposals would make it illegal to treat people differently on the grounds of age, for example in recruitment, selection and promotion decisions, unless employers and others with obligations can justify such differential treatment with reference to specific aims and produce supporting evidence. *Equality and Diversity* also suggests that retirement ages set for employees by their employers would be prohibited, except in exceptional circumstances.[27]

Health

Ageing is clearly an important factor in anticipating the cost of healthcare. People aged over 65 currently account for one-third of spending on hospital and community health services.[28] However, the issue of ageing and health costs is more complicated than it appears. The costs of health and social care do increase with age but, as Metz argues, the most substantial requirement for health and social care occurs in the final year or two of life, regardless of the age of death.[29] The proportion of an age cohort that is dying increases with age, giving the impression that healthcare costs rise as well. But, since we can die only once, the overall cost of a person's healthcare over their lifetime will not necessarily increase very much. In fact there are a number of reasons to think that the proportion of a person's total healthcare cost accounted for because people live longer may fall as a result of a set of effects known as the 'compression of morbidity', outlined below. That said, the size of the baby boomer cohort will mean that the Treasury will have to pay a greater number of expensive health bills simultaneously (probably during the 2030s), which will increase fiscal pressures at that time.[30]

In 2001, the Chancellor commissioned Derek Wanless to examine 'the technological, demographic and medical trends over the next two decades that may affect the health service in the UK as a whole'. In light of these findings he was 'to identify the key factors which will determine the financial and other resources required to ensure that the NHS can provide a publicly funded, comprehensive, high quality service available on the basis of clinical need and not ability to pay'.

The Wanless Report was published in the spring of 2002. It suggested that to meet changing demands for healthcare NHS spending would need to rise from around £68 billion in 2002/3 to £154–184 billion in 2022/3. Among the factors driving these increases, the report argued that it was likely that 'future older people will be increasingly intolerant of any differential access to services. They are likely to be more demanding of the health service, thanks to greater awareness of health and available interventions.'[31]

The Chancellor agreed with the report's forecasts, and in the 2002 Budget announced major increases in long-term health spending. Spending would increase by 7.4 per cent in real terms for each of the next five years, leading to an increase in the total NHS budget from £65.4 billion in 2002/3 to £105.6 billion in 2007/8, or as a proportion of GDP from 7.7 per cent in 2002/3 to 9.4 per cent in 2007/8.[32]

Alongside this investment, the government has sought to reform the way the health service operates. Providing a more effective service to older citizens is one aspect of this. In the National Service Framework for Older People, published in March 2001, the government claimed to offer for the first time 'a 10 year programme of action linking services to support independence and promote good health, specialised services for key conditions, and culture change so that all older people and their carers are always treated with respect, dignity and fairness'. The result, it claimed, would be the first 'comprehensive strategy to ensure fair, high quality, integrated health and social care services for older people'. [33]

Long-term care

When the new Labour government came into power in 1997 there was a widespread feeling that the implications of an ageing society for the provision and financing of long-term care for older people needed urgently to be addressed. In December 1997 the government set up the Royal Commission on Long Term Care for the Elderly.

The Royal Commission drew a distinction between personal and nursing care, but could not agree on how they should be financed. The majority report suggested that both should be funded by the state, while the minority report argued that the state should only fund nursing care. Controversially, the UK government decided to reject the view of the majority report and sided with the minority report. However, in Scotland, where social care was a devolved matter, the Scottish Parliament agreed to the majority report's recommendation, causing considerable embarrassment to the government in London.

The issue turned on the affordability of personal and nursing care in an ageing society. The majority report took the view that any analysis of the cost of care needed to take into account growth in the economy as a whole. So although long-term care expenditure was expected to triple, in real terms (as a proportion of GDP) it would remain relatively steady, only rising by 0.3 per cent of GDP from 1995 to 2051[34] (see table 2.2).

While the government rejected the commission's recommendation to consider the creation of an integrated health and social care system for older people, it committed itself to effective partnership working between those services.[35] It accepted the recommendation that 'care in the home so far as this is feasible should be available for as long as

Table 2.2 Projections of spending on long-term care in the UK

Year	Spending on long-term care in the UK	
	(£bn)	(% of GDP)
1995	11.1	1.6
2010	14.7	1.5
2021	19.9	1.6
2031	28.0	1.8
2051	45.3	1.9

Source: Royal Commission on Long Term Care for the Elderly, *With Respect to Old Age: long term care – rights and responsibilities*

possible'. The extension of healthy life expectancy through the promotion of a health and active life in old age is also one of the main aims of the government's National Service Framework for Older People for the NHS.[36]

A more recent problem is growing fear of a crisis in the care home market. In the UK, in 2001 more than 13,000 residential care places for the elderly – the large majority of them in the independent sector – were lost.[37] Such closures have highlighted a number of crucial tensions in the system. One problem is funding: in 2002 research for the Joseph Rowntree Foundation found that the care home sector was currently underfunded by £1 billion a year. [38] In part this is due to the purchasing power of local authorities, which allows them to drive down prices. Faced with comparatively low returns on their investment, many care home owners have also been tempted to sell up in order to cash in on a booming property market. Finally, there has been some debate about the extent to which government demands for minimum standards of care enforced through regulations have impacted on the number of places, and whether care home owners have chosen exit ahead of compliance.[39]

The limits of the current approach

Our aim here is not to question or dispute the significance of these issues. On the contrary, we take it as self-evident that they are crucially important. Yet a central question remains about how they might come to be resolved. There can be little doubt that demographic change on this kind of scale cannot readily be absorbed by the existing cultures and institutions of our society – whether in welfare, work, health or long-term care – without in the process forcing them to undergo far-reaching changes in their organising principles and modes of delivery. Nor is it possible to envisage how the transition to a new set of arrangements might be negotiated without taking into account the kinds of values and value change required to support and legitimate it.

For example the impact that an ageing society will have on health spending greatly depends on the significance of the 'compression of morbidity' – the idea that as well as living longer lives, we will also stay healthier for longer. This effect is expected to lower health and long-term care costs for older generations in the future compared with today. The evidence itself is unclear: research suggests that older people are experiencing fewer severe (acute) health problems and a corresponding increase in long-term chronic conditions.[40] Research in the US found some evidence of the compression of morbidity already happening.[41] In the Wanless review, uncertainty about the existence or size of the effect was one reason for the wide disparities in projected costs across his three scenarios, which by 2022/3 could represent as much as £30 billion.[42] But which scenario or combination of scenarios will be realised will depend on how successfully we can create a healthcare infrastructure that actively encourages, motivates and enables preventative action by its citizen users.

Similarly, the real implications of the pensions shortfall will be determined by how effectively adjustments can be made in other areas of social and economic activity: in how long people are willing, and able, to carry on working; in the kinds of financial services products they are prepared to invest in; in the ways that government can find to support and compensate the valued social activities like caring that older people carry out; and so on.

And just as important as whether or not long-term care is affordable is the question of how it is to be organised. How will the current tension between regulating the quality and increasing the availability of care be overcome? How will the respective rights and responsibilities of individuals, their families or the state to pay and provide for it be determined? How will family life be supported and nurtured in an ageing society?

What all these examples illustrate is the futility of trying to 'read across' from a set of abstract population projections to a coherent picture of what the world will actually look like in 2050. In each case, people's behaviours and the attitudes and values that underpin them are at least as important to how different aspects of the transition to later life are negotiated as the raw demographic numbers.

We need to take a different starting point. We must begin by looking at tomorrow's older generation, at who they are, what they think and why that makes them so important.

To sum up:

- The headline figures for the scale of the demographic transition are dramatic.
- These figures have led to a very negative policy agenda focused on those policy areas where the status quo is most threatened, rather than on imagining entirely new sets of arrangements.
- The main concerns revolve around pensions, work, health and long-term care.
- In each case, the raw numbers tell only part of the story, because so much of how the issue will play out depends on other factors – not least the attitudes and values of the people making the transition themselves.

- Trying to 'read across' from a set of abstract population projections to a coherent picture of what the world will actually look like on its own is futile. We have to consider much more seriously the values and attitudes that the baby boomers will carry into the transition.

3. Introducing the 'new old'

Who are the baby boomers?

In this pamphlet, we define the baby boomers as the generation born between 1945 and 1965. During this time some 18.5 million children were born in the UK, with two peaks in the birth rate in 1947 and 1964[43] (see figure 3.1). Today there are around 17 million baby boomers in the UK, making up approximately 29 per cent of the total population.[44]

As a generation, baby boomers have lived through a period of rapid and intense change and shared a set of formative influences and experiences – including the absence of large-scale military conflict, the creation of a cradle-to-grave welfare state, the 'sexual revolution', the introduction of mass education and the emergence of the consumer society – which are distinctly different from those of their parents.

Yet to try to define, even in the broadest terms, what makes a particular generation distinctive is not only difficult but, if it leads us towards the kind of easy generalisations that are often made about current generations of older people, also potentially dangerous. Nevertheless, we believe it is worth attempting to do this. In the first place, we think there are some general points that can be made about the baby boomers as a generation that are worth stating here. But perhaps more importantly, the baby boomers are widely seen as a *vanguard* generation; they have not just experienced these various

Figure 3.1 UK birth rates 1930–1995: 1940s and 1960s booms

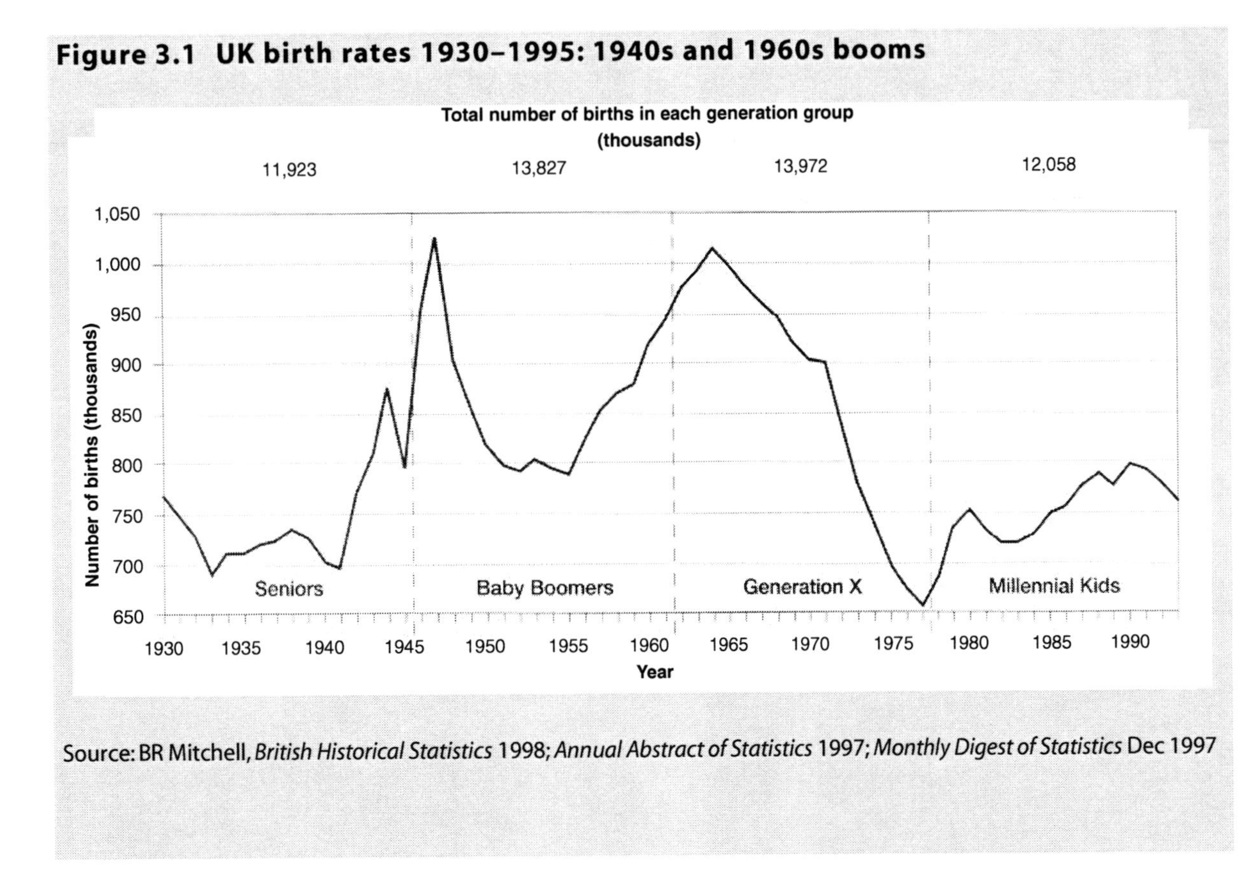

Source: BR Mitchell, *British Historical Statistics* 1998; *Annual Abstract of Statistics* 1997; *Monthly Digest of Statistics* Dec 1997

social transformations as they have passed through different life stages, but actively instigated them. To the extent that this image matches the reality, it is clear that clarifying and interrogating the evidence of the baby boomers' underlying *value base* is crucial to understanding how their transition to later life will play out. Of course, though we are critical of the idea that the characteristics of older people remain fixed from one generation to the next, we recognise the danger of substituting this stereotype for a new caricature of the baby boomers as an entire generation of rebellious, anti-establishment '68ers'. Indeed, we suggest that one of the defining features of the baby boom generation may, paradoxically, be that it is so difficult to define – that it is so fragmented in terms of the attitudes and values of different groups within the cohort.

Common ground

The baby boomers are renowned for two distinctive generational characteristics, individualism and liberalism, and from our analysis of the attitudinal data it is clear that these characteristics do stand out.

Individualism

The baby boomers are often said to be very individualistic (some might even say egotistical), an image which stands in stark juxtaposition to that of their parents' generation who – largely because of the experience of the Second World War – are seen to put much greater emphasis on collective solidarity, evoked in phrases like the 'Dunkirk spirit' and 'Blitz mentality'.

This individualism rests on a number of bases. First, it involves a distinctive orientation away from formal authority, bolstered by their association with various 1960s countercultures and their distrust of 'the establishment' in its various cultural and institutional guises. Even today baby boomers are:

- *More anti-establishment* 19 per cent of baby boomers claim that they do not feel part of the British system, compared with 11 per cent of those aged 55 and over.

- *More non-conformist* They are the least likely of any age group to agree that it is important to fit in rather than be different from other people.[45] Only 7 per cent of early Boomers, those born between 1945 and 1955, think it is important that people admire the things they own, compared with 13 per cent of pre-Boomers and 20 per cent of post-Boomers.[46]
- *Less deferential* Only 14 per cent of baby boomers believe that 'the people in charge know best', compared with 20 per cent of the younger and 26 per cent of the older generation.[47]
- *Less trusting of those in authority* 69.5 per cent of baby boomers do not think that politicians are trustworthy, compared with 60 per cent of the older generation. 36.5 per cent of baby boomers do not think senior public service managers are trustworthy, compared with 26.5 per cent of the older generation.[48]
- *More hostile to organised religion* Only 27 per cent of baby boomers think that 'people who don't believe in God have something important missing in their lives', half the figure for those aged 55 and over.[49]

That baby boomers have retained this anti-establishment feeling as they have aged is ironic since to all intents and purposes they now are the establishment. Just how individual this individualism really is, how much it is about *being different* rather than just *being seen to be different*, is debatable. What seems more likely is that it is consistent with a second aspect of the baby boomers' individualism, namely their experience of *consumerism*, which permits precisely this kind of reconciliation between the desire to make ever more personalised choices and the need to remain within homogenised systems for managing them. The baby boomers are the first generation to have grown up in a consumer society: to be products of the age of affluence; to have been advertised and marketed to all their lives; to have come to expect their individual wants and needs to be satisfied;

to have been encouraged to define themselves by the personal choices they make about what to wear, buy, eat or watch. Where their parents had rationing, the baby boomers had the TV dinner.

Today, the baby boomer generation overall is the most economically powerful section of UK society. Not only do baby boomers earn more than any other age group,[50] they also own more assets; for example, they are the largest group of owner-occupiers in Britain.[51] As the pioneers of the consumer society, the baby boomers today constitute a unique generation of what we might call 'smart' consumers. They are aware of their choices and highly sensitive to being patronised. They have been advertised to all their lives, and have retained a particularly rational and practical relationship to brands: they are brand literate, but not brand dependent:

- Only 11 per cent of early baby boomers, those born between 1945 and 1955, and 24 per cent of late boomers, those born between 1956 and 1965, agreed with the statement 'I like products with designer names on them.' This compares with 55 per cent of the younger generation agreeing with this statement.[52]
- Baby boomers are less likely than younger or older generations to measure their success by the things they own.[53]

Baby boomers are the least likely to 'generally spend extra for a brand with the right image'.[54]

The importance of this individual streak is fourfold. First, it highlights the extent to which the baby boomers may be the first generation of older people for whom an understanding of the good life may be framed in explicitly consumerist terms, with all the contradictions that might imply. For example, the success of BMW's new Mini, and Volkswagen's resurrected and redesigned Campervan, has been widely attributed to baby boomers buying into 1960s and 1970s nostalgia.[55] Yet arguably the sector that has responded most swiftly and effectively to the baby boomers' ageing is the beauty industry (including cosmetics and plastic surgery), which has already profited massively from well-off baby boomers' desire to stay young.[56]

Second, it sheds new light on the (often heated) debate about whether the users of public services should be thought of as 'citizens' or 'consumers'.[57] Over the last decade, there has been a trend towards thinking about the users of public services as consumers,[58] and an associated interest in applying concepts such as choice and competition to the reform of those services.[59] The argument runs that citizens increasingly expect to have the same levels of choice, customisation and quality in public services as they would expect in the private sector, and there is some evidence that for the baby boomers this may be true. 60.5 per cent claim one of the most important factors in shaping their trust in public services is 'whether it meets their needs', compared with 49 per cent of the older generation.[60]

Third, it suggests that consumerism could form the basis of the baby boomers' political activity in a way that it has not for earlier generations. Baby boomers have pioneered ethical consumption, with 23 per cent having boycotted a company's product on ethical grounds, compared with only 13 per cent of the older generation. 20 per cent of Boomers have positively chosen to buy a product or service because of the company's ethical reputation.[61] Potentially the most important development could be the growing popularity of ethical investment in financial service products, although it is not yet clear how potent an instrument for change this will prove to be in practice.

Fourth, it underlines the importance of governing the transition in a way that works with rather than against the grain of this individualism, and which respects and harnesses the kinds of personal choices that it implies. As Tom Bentley has argued, this is a serious challenge for many of the institutions through which modern social, economic and political life is organised, which have come to depend on forms of command-and-control intervention ill-suited to an environment in which individual freedom, choice and autonomy is so highly prized.[62]

Liberalism

Another article of faith is that the baby boomers are a greatly more liberal generation than their parents.

The first and perhaps most salient dimension of this surrounds personal lifestyle choices and the extent to which these should remain personal. The baby boomers are seen, depending on your point of view, either as the vanguard of the 'sexual revolution' or as the architects of the 'permissive society'. The development of the contraceptive pill and the reform of divorce and abortion law all took place on the baby boomers' watch, and made a lasting impression on their attitudes and values. So baby boomers take a more liberal view than their parents on:

- *Sex before marriage* 59.5 per cent of baby boomers think there is nothing wrong with in a man and woman having sex before marriage, more than double the number of those aged 55 and over.[63]
- *Having children outside wedlock* Only 43 per cent of baby boomers think that 'people who want children ought to get married', while among the older generation almost double the number, 80.5 per cent, think that they should.[64]
- *Cohabitation* 76.5 per cent of baby boomers agree that 'it is all right for a couple to live together without intending to get married', compared with just 46 per cent among the older generation.[65]
- *Homosexuality* 35 per cent of younger baby boomers, those born between 1956 and 1965, and 20 per cent of older baby boomers, those born between 1945 and 1955, say it is 'not wrong at all' for two adults of the same sex to have sexual relations, compared with just 9 per cent of over 65s.[66]
- *Sexual mores* Around 47 per cent of baby boomers attribute teenage pregnancy to 'a lack of morals among young people', compared with 74.5 per cent of those aged 55 and over.[67]

But alongside this libertarian strand, the baby boomers' liberalism also extends to the political or public sphere. The baby boomers have been at the forefront of many of the progressive social movements of the last 50 years, from anti-racism and 'women's lib' to the green movement. This has shaped their attitudes and values today: only 15.4 per cent of baby boomers agree with the statement that 'when it comes down to it, the man's job is to be the breadwinner and the woman's is to look after the home'. Among the over-55 age group, however, the figure for those who agree to that statement is more than twice that at 38.9 per cent.[68] 16 per cent of baby boomers see 'Pollution/Environment' as one of the main issues facing Britain today,[69] compared with just 4 per cent of the older generation.

Boomers also take a more liberal line on illegal drugs than earlier generations, with 45.5 per cent of baby boomers supporting the legalisation of cannabis and 27 per cent claiming to have used it. By contrast, just 4 per cent of the older generation have used cannabis themselves and only 27 per cent think it should be legalised.[70]

Finally, the baby boomers' liberalism means that they tend to be more internationalist in their outlook, with 35 per cent of baby boomers feeling 'that they are more a citizen of the world than a citizen of their country'. This compares with 29 per cent of the older generation having this view.[71] This liberalism also manifests itself in their reading of global geopolitics. The baby boomers are distinctively both more anti-American and more pro-European than older generations, no doubt in part because of the differential impact of their formative experiences (such as Vietnam) compared with those of their parents:

- While almost one-third (29 per cent) of older generations believe that 'The US should remain the only superpower' only one-sixth (16 per cent) of baby boomers agree.[72]
- 58 per cent of baby boomers agree that 'The European Union should become a superpower, like the United States'; only 45 per cent of older generations agreed with this statement.[73]

Figure 3.2 The baby boom generation

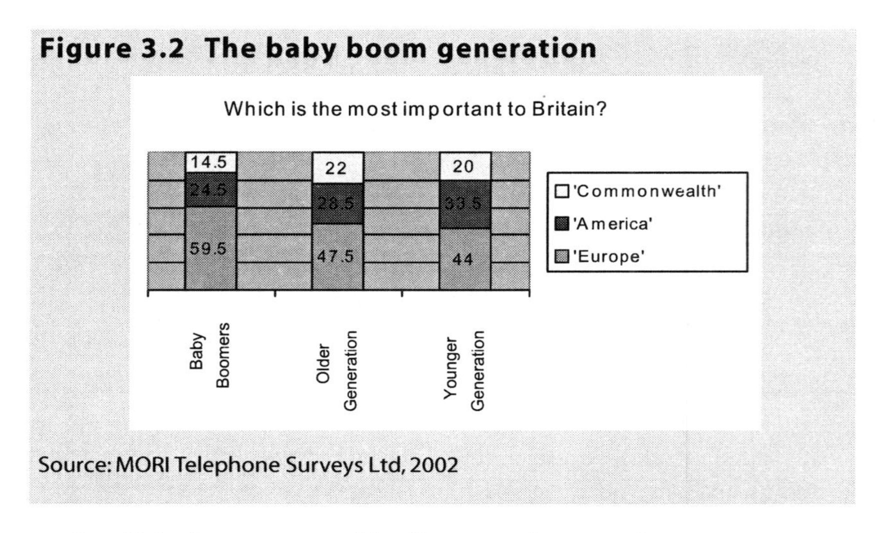

Source: MORI Telephone Surveys Ltd, 2002

- Baby boomers consider Europe to be more important to Britain and the US and the Commonwealth less important to Britain than either older or younger generations (see figure 3.2)

The baby boomers' liberalism is important because of the impact that it has already had on reshaping and reconfiguring the personal circumstances of the baby boom generation, and because of its potential impact on shaping their demands in the future. In terms of the former, there are clear implications for family structure and, by extension, for a whole series of systems and institutions whose viability is predicated on that structure remaining stable. In the welfare arena, for example, a spouse or partner is typically the most important source of support for older people in need of care, yet between 40 and 50 per cent of baby boomers are likely to be 'living solo' by the age of 75.[74] It also reinforces the importance of creating public services that treat people equally, irrespective of race, religion or colour: 49.5 per cent of baby boomers see this as one of the most significant factors in determining how much they trust public services, compared with just 36 per cent of older generations.[75]

The direct implications at this stage for public services are much less clear, although some possibilities are emerging. Given the importance of global issues like climate change over the next 50 years, it may well be the internationalist dimension of the baby boomers' liberalism that becomes most crucial in years to come. Is it difficult to conceive of new, libertarian rallying cries emerging around the primacy of personal choice. In recent years the issue of euthanasia has assumed a more prominent position in public and media debates following these high-profile cases: an unnamed solicitor who suffered brain-damage while recovering from a minor operation granted the right to die by the High Court in 2001, Diane Pretty and Reginald Crewe who were denied the right to die in 2002, and most recently Robert and Jennifer Stokes, who were helped to commit suicide in Zurich by the Swiss charity Dignitas. The attitudinal data suggests that the proportion in favour of the 'right to die' could be reaching a critical mass, with 65 per cent of baby boomers saying that they would like to be able to bring about their own death peacefully when they feel it's time, compared with 53 per cent of the older age group and 61 per cent of the younger generation.[76]

Figure 3.3 summarises the portrait of the baby boom generation this chapter has sought to paint so far.

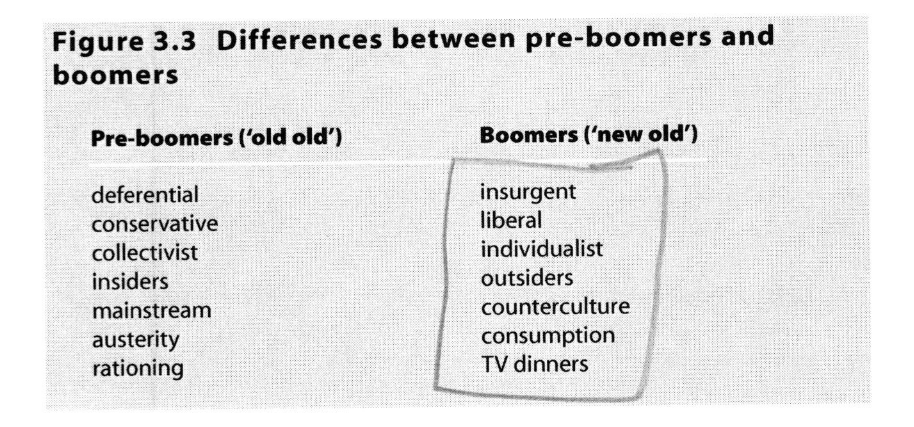

Figure 3.3 Differences between pre-boomers and boomers

Pre-boomers ('old old')	Boomers ('new old')
deferential	insurgent
conservative	liberal
collectivist	individualist
insiders	outsiders
mainstream	counterculture
austerity	consumption
rationing	TV dinners

A divided generation?

Yet beneath this veneer of homogeneity there are deep divisions within the baby boom generation. In fact, although their parents are certainly not homogeneous either, one of the defining features of the baby boomers is that they are arguably the most diverse and divided generation to have reached this point in life. The most important differences include:

- age and formative influences
- wealth
- longevity
- education
- gender
- ethnicity
- politics.

Age and formative influences

The first and most obvious division is that baby boomers' formative influences (particularly in the transition to adulthood) have been effectively polarised by a marked reversal in Britain's economic fortunes. As a result it is often appropriate to divide them into two cohorts – the early baby boomers born between 1945 and 1955, and the late baby boomers born from 1956 to 1965.

The early baby boomers, although initially born into a period of postwar austerity, entered the labour market in a period of relative economic prosperity. Along with a buoyant job market, they were also the first beneficiaries of the rapid expansion of higher education.[77] By contrast, the experience of the late baby boomers was markedly less positive, as Evandrou evocatively describes and figure 3.4 illustrates:

> [the late baby boomers] were born into a period of prosperity – experiencing the consumer spending boom of the 1960s and comprehensive secondary education. But by the time they came

> to enter the labour market at the end of the 1970s, the economy was entering a recession, resulting in sharp rises in unemployment... Some of this group have never had a permanent full-time job. The spirit of radicalism and freedom, enjoyed by the preceding baby boom cohort, was missing...1984 saw the first person diagnosed with AIDS, and so marked the end of the sexual revolution. In contrast with the 1960s, the 1980s were symbolised by the rise of the 'yuppie' and the imperatives of the private sector.[78]

Figure 3.4 Formative influences on baby boomers

1950s:
Benefiting from introduction of comprehensive secondary education and NHS
Onset of television age

1960s:
Berlin Wall built
Economic growth and consumer spending boom
Rapid expansion of higher education
Protest movements – Vietnam, feminism, race relations, gay rights
Rock, Beatles, drug culture, flower power
Liberal legislation on abortion and homosexuality
Pill available on NHS
First moon landing

1970s:
Divorce reform Act implemented
Environmental movement, CND
OPEC crisis
Winter of Discontent
Margaret Thatcher elected
Recession and high unemployment

1980s:
80s boom
Aids
Live Aid
Retreat of welfare state and privatisation
Divorce and family breakdown
Black Monday, house price crash
Health and fitness boom
Berlin Wall falls

1990s:
Thatcher resigns
Black Wednesday
Tony Blair 'New Labour' elected

Age: 70, 60, 50, 40, 30, 20, 10

Source: adapted version of table from the Henley Centre, 2002

These very different experiences have affected and influenced the respective generations of baby boomers' and their lives, and created two quite distinct baby boomer cohorts with often separate or even contradictory attitudes and values. So, for example, the late baby boomers are typically:

- less internationalist in outlook than early baby boomers, feeling less in touch with what is happening in other parts of the world, and less a citizen of the world or part of the global village[79]
- more supportive of multiculturalism[80]
- more liberal in their attitudes to marriage, premarital sex, homosexuality or having children outside wedlock.[81]

Wealth

As well as this horizontal division, the baby boom generation is criss-crossed by a set of vertical cleavages and divisions running right though the cohort, which militate against simply dividing them into early or late groups. Not least among these is affluence. The baby boomers' association with consumerism is not just sociological but also economic. They are currently the most economically powerful section of society, and they have the highest average income and expenditure in the population.[82] Yet the emphasis that is placed on consumer power serves to perpetuate and reinforce a conception of the baby boomer as an inherently middle-class construct, combining a progressive liberal agenda on social issues with an unprecedented appetite and capacity for personal consumption. This conception largely ignores the large segment of the baby boom generation for whom this middle-class identity does not fit at all well, namely:

- the 8 per cent of baby boomers who earn less than £250 per week[83]
- the 3.5 per cent who are unemployed (according to the ILO) and have no work-related earnings at all[84]
- the 20 per cent who have no private pension and plan to rely entirely on state provision.[85]

Longevity

These differences in wealth are matched by differences in longevity. Although life expectancy overall has greatly increased, differences in longevity by social class have not narrowed in 30 years. Someone born in 1946, at the beginning of the baby boom, was expected to live to 65.8 years.[86] A baby boomer aged 50 in 1999 could be expected to live more than ten years beyond that estimate, to an average age of 77.7 years. However, there is a marked divergence in longevity according to social class. Even at age 65, when the major differences in infant mortality have been factored out of the life expectancy calculation, a man from social class I (professional) can expect to live until 82.5 years and a man from social class V (unskilled manual) until 78.4 years.[87]

Education

The same goes for education. Overall, baby boomers, and particularly women, are much more educated than their parents' generation. 27.5 per cent of baby boomer men and 24.5 per cent of baby boomer women have a degree or equivalent or have been in higher education (below degree level). In contrast, 25 per cent of the male older generation and 37 per cent of the female older generation had no qualifications at all. However, these relatively high levels of attainment compared with earlier generations serve to exacerbate inequalities of attainment within the cohort. Despite the good performance at the top end of the scale, 14 per cent of male baby boomers and 20.5 per cent of female baby boomers have no qualifications at all.

Gender

Gender remains an important source of differentiation running through these other divisions. Most obviously, the pay gap between male and female baby boomers remains severe. The median annual income for women hovers at around 60 per cent of the median annual income for men across the cohort.[88] Similarly, while 59 per cent of baby boomer men have a degree or equivalent, have been in higher education (below degree level), or have a GCE A-level or equivalent, only 38 per cent of women have any of these three educational qualifications.[89]

Ethnicity

Finally, a further source of heterogeneity is that the baby boomers are significantly more culturally and ethnically diverse than their parents' generation. The beginning of the baby boom coincided with a period of mass migration from former British colonies after the Second World War. As a result, there are over a million ethnic minority baby boomers, making up approximately 5.5 per cent of the generation. In contrast, there are approximately 320,000 people from ethnic minority groups aged 60 or over, or around 1 per cent of this age group.[90] This is potentially very important in thinking about long-term care, for example, in that family roles and structures (both real and perceived) vary between ethnic groups and between generations within ethnic groups. Government must therefore be sensitive to these multicultural perspectives and nuances in considering what the most appropriate policy response should be.

Politics

Finally, the baby boomers' distinctive history does not translate into support for one political party over another. This runs counter to the conventional wisdom that the ageing of the baby boomers will benefit parties on the centre-left and hurt parties on the right. Underpinning this position tends to be the idea that the baby boomers are more educated and, so the argument runs, therefore more liberal than any older generation before them.[91]

It is true that baby boomers currently lean marginally to the left. 45 per cent of baby boomers identify with Labour, compared with 42 per cent of younger generations and 40.5 per cent of older generations, and a slightly higher proportion of baby boomers vote Labour than in the population as a whole.[92]

But these differences are fairly marginal, and may be offset by the fact that people have historically tended to shift to the right as they get older, while Labour support remains relatively constant across all age groups.[93] Perhaps more worrying for the Conservative Party is the existence of a seemingly significant generational disjunction between the baby boomers and older generations that is not so much pro-Labour as it is anti-Tory. While 40.5 per cent of those aged 55 and over identify with the Conservatives, only 24.5 per cent of baby boomers (and 15.5 per cent of 18 to 34-year-olds) do.[94] However, these figures must also be interpreted in the context of falling electoral turnout and long-term decline in party identification across all age groups, which has led to a much more fluid electoral environment.[95] For the time being, at least, it seems safe to assume that older voters will remain as divided as they have always been.

Figure 3.5 summarises some of the key differences between the baby boomers as a sociocultural construct and the baby boomers as an age cohort.

The contours of a new approach

The portrait that emerges is therefore of a generation that in terms of its size and character will be quite unlike any that went before it. But at the same time this latticework of cleavages carries with it the potential to unite or divide the baby boom generation on a whole

Figure 3.5 Differences between baby boomers as a sociocultural construct and as an age cohort

Boomers as sociocultural construct	Boomers as age cohort
Homogeneity	Heterogeneity
Middle-class	Major class differentials
68ers	Mixed motifs (e.g. Yuppie)
Monoculturalism	Multiculturalism
Affluence	Income inequality
Highly educated	Many poorly qualified
Gender equality	Persistent gender inequality
Sexual revolution	AIDS generation

series of issues, even if the nature of the clusters that will develop, or the particular societal cleavages that will become most salient, remains unclear for the time being. To understand a generation of individualists, we need to look in much more detail at the interface between attitudinal change and the different contexts, institutions and practices it will affect. That means marshalling what we know about values and the way they change over the lifetime, notably the impact of:

- *Life-cycle (chronological) effects* People's attitudes tend to differ at different points in their lives – engagement in politics follows a classic life-cycle. Younger generations have always been less interested in politics and the older people get, the more politically involved they generally become. Moreover, attitudes on social spending also tend to be affected by life-cycle changes. Older people place higher importance on pension and health spending, whereas younger people tend to emphasise educational spending.
- *Period (societal) effects* Events occur that influence attitudes across the whole of society. Changes in our attitudes towards the environment result from period effects as in recent years all sections of society have become more environmentally friendly.
- *Cohort (generational) effects* These are a distinctive set of attitudes or behaviour patterns among a cohort that the cohort tends to adhere to as it grows older. Religiosity would be a model cohort effect. Younger generations are less religious than their predecessors and will not become more religious as they age. More liberal attitudes towards premarital sex as well as homosexuality also result from cohort effects.

We are conscious of Jowell's warning about 'gee whiz' analysis, 'which reveals striking differences between older and younger people on a particular measure and then just leaves it to the reader to say "gee whiz!" and perhaps to draw all sorts of heroic conclusions'.[96] Avoiding this tendency fully requires intensive longitudinal analysis, which remains beyond the scope of this pamphlet, but which an ongoing strand of Demos work will seek to generate over the coming year.

Nevertheless, the evidence also shows that there are some core beliefs that carry through. Ronald Inglehart has famously described a shift from a 'materialist' to a 'post-materialist' politics across many developed countries driven by precisely this kind of underlying value change.[97] Given what we know about the baby boomers' underlying values, it seems plausible as a working hypothesis that they will coalesce into one of three categories:

- *The Selfish Generation* A generation of individualists, and pioneers of the consumer society, will unite around the pursuit of their own fulfilment and the enjoyment of their accumulated wealth as their overarching goal, with little regard for the needs of less well-off contemporaries or future generations.
- *The Civic Defenders* A generation of liberal activists will act as a civic bulwark against the erosion of the public realm (which in some ways their individualism and consumerism helped to unleash), creating the conditions for a radical and progressive politics.
- *The Invisible Elders* A fragmented generation will fail to coalesce at all, and have little or no collective influence. It will splinter into a range of much smaller sub-categories, which will be absorbed into other currents of social change, and define themselves through forms of identity distinct from their age cohort.

But even if the clusters of values that will group the baby boomers have not yet crystallised, we can begin to cluster the emerging issues. In the chapters that follow we pursue this line of argument, scanning across a broad spectrum of social life to focus on three sets of issues that seem prominent and pressing. They are:

- the way baby boomers want to define their later life and their priorities for self-fulfilment
- the importance of participation in and engagement with the communities and the environments to which they belong, and how this impacts on their quality of life
- intergenerational equity, and their relationship with other generations.

To sum up:

- The baby boomers' generation is very different from those that have gone before it.
- Two particularly important characteristics are baby boomers' individualism and their liberalism.
- The baby boomers do not conform to any single stereotype any more than earlier generations have. There are significant differences between them in affluence, longevity, education and ethnicity.
- This underlines the importance of establishing a distinction between baby boomers as a highly heterogeneous, fragmented cohort, and baby boomers as a homogeneous, cultural construct.
- Although the groups of values around which baby boomers will group are unclear, it is possible to identify some salient clusters of issues.

4. From retirement to reordering: baby boomers' priorities for self-fulfilment, and how they can be supported

> *There has always been some kind of sense that, if people survive in retirement, the experience that is embodied in them can be very socially useful. And a lot of structures are such that they don't allow this to happen.*
>
> Male baby boomer

Later life has long been defined by what it is *not*. This is reflected in the language we use – the word 'retirement' reinforces the idea that later life is about *not* working, but offers little by way of a more positive image of what it could represent or offer. Yet it is increasingly clear that later life is a distinct life stage in itself, and to view it as the twilight of a career beyond which meaningful self-fulfilment becomes impossible is simply inadequate. Instead, we need to think about how a generation of older people that is healthier, more highly educated and living longer lives than any that has gone before it will wish to define and pursue a broader notion of quality of life.

But one of the paradoxes of the ageing society is that, just as demographic change makes it both more possible and more essential to develop this more positive and more rounded conception of what later life means, the policy agenda is becoming more preoccupied than ever with perpetuating the traditional polarisation between work and retirement.

At the root of the problem seems to be a particular notion of what a normal working life should look like. We might call this the '20/40/10 conception': learn for 20 years, work for 40 years, rest and play for 10 years. Over the last 20 years this 20/40/10 model has been undermined by rapid social and economic change: rising longevity, lower levels of employment among older age groups and the declining performance of stock-market-based pension funds not least among them. Yet rather than abandon this notion completely policy-makers have engaged in increasingly desperate attempts to preserve it, stretching it to fit changing circumstances. The focus has been on finding the means to encourage people to work longer and retire later or, to put it another way, on lengthening the 40 in order to pay for the 10.

This polarisation of employment–retirement, work–play is unhelpful for all sorts of reasons. In particular, it negates the whole concept and vocabulary of the 'work–life balance', and fails to recognise that the key to quality of life will not be the satisfaction of any one set of material needs, but rather the quality of the experiences that older people are able to enjoy and the way that these can be combined and reconciled. For some baby boomers, this may involve a new career direction; for others it entails the exercise of consumer power or the discharge of caring responsibilities for grandchildren. Whatever the specific priorities, this chapter argues that we need a new framework and a set of policy instruments that grants baby boomers as much freedom and autonomy as possible about how they identify and support their quality of life, and about the roles that they are allowed to fulfil in doing so.

Context

Work has been the early warning system of the ageing society. The notion of the demographic 'time bomb' largely grew out of a better understanding of the changing age composition of the labour force, a trend that foreshadowed more wide-reaching challenges further down the line once these numbers had filtered through into the dependency ratio.

In chapter 2, we saw how the overall thrust of the political response to this ageing workforce has largely been one of damage limitation. The focus has been on encouraging people to work longer in order to finance their retirement, through a process of creating incentives and opportunities and removing barriers.

Many of these courses of action are to be welcomed, notably the focus on helping those whose early exit from the labour market is prompted by age discrimination or a lack of certain workplace skills. However, such measures are underpinned by a set of assumptions that are much less helpful in defining the nature and scope of the political task. The three most important of these hypotheses are that the problem:

- is about pensions, and whether individuals have saved enough or whether they need to work longer, rather than about the baby boomers' self-fulfilment and quality of life in a more positive sense
- is an issue that only affects certain people (namely those without a big enough pension), rather than being about extending choice and autonomy as widely as possible, and creating the legitimacy for those choices to be exercised
- can and should be dealt with in isolation from other issues, without needing take into account other forms of socioeconomic activity and need (such as childcare).

But by preserving these assumptions we are in danger of:

- failing to take into account what we know about the baby boomers' past and current behaviour and attitudes in this area
- causing resentment and hostility within and between generations
- excluding other problems that any potential solutions need to take into account

- ignoring the extent to which work not only enables us to satisfy material needs but also contributes to our sense of identity, happiness and fulfilment.

Let us consider each of these in turn.

Baby boomers and work

Baby boomers have pioneered new kinds of working practices all their lives and the hallmark of many of these innovations has been flexibility. Boomers have helped to engineer a shift from the full-time 'job for life' towards more flexible forms of employment including part-time and temporary work, fixed-term contracts and 'portfolio' careers. More than one-quarter of baby boomers are currently in 'atypical' forms of employment (self-employed or part-time).[98]

One of the main reasons for this trend is that more than earlier generations, baby boomers value the ability to combine different kinds of activity and to achieve a reasonable work–life balance. Today:

- 78.5 per cent of baby boomers agree strongly or tend to agree that 'although I enjoy my work, my private life is more important to me', compared with only 44 per cent of those aged 55 and over.[99]
- 66 per cent of baby boomers agree strongly or tend to agree that 'if work interferes with my personal life, I would put it into second place', compared with only 45 per cent of those aged 55 and over.[100]
- 49.5 per cent of baby boomers 'resent overtime eating into their free time, even if it is paid', compared with 42 per cent of those aged 55.[101]

As they enter later life, baby boomers are likely to be deeply hostile to any attempt to encourage them to work longer unless it works with the grain of their desire for flexibility in the way work is organised, in the level of time commitment involved, and in how it is structured to dovetail with other activities and responsibilities. In other words, it seems that the key issue is going to be greater flexibility not in when retirement begins but in what it is allowed to mean, and the range of different activities that can be accommodated.

Resentment, solidarity and trust

It seems clear that some people will need to work longer to make up for expected shortfall in their pension provision. In this group, those on lower incomes, women and people from ethnic minorities will be disproportionately represented.[102] But the danger is that by focusing solely on this section of society, and on the need to provide members of these groups with the means to improve their own financial security, we increase the antagonism and resentment that they feel towards the better-off within their age cohort and also towards a state that (they may feel) has failed to protect their 'entitlement' to a proper retirement.

What this means, in other words, is that the problem cannot fully be resolved unless we can transform not just the behaviour of those individuals who are particularly affected by it, but also the underlying social norms about what a 'normal' pattern of working life looks like. For this new settlement to gain legitimacy, and for the government to retain public trust, the focus of policy needs to shift in two ways.

First, the need for individuals to make good these shortfalls will breed a great deal less resentment if government and employers were to accept by way of a *quid pro quo* the need for these final years in work to be as effectively customised to the needs of the individual employee as possible. This might mean working fewer or more flexible hours, or engaging in different kinds of work.

Second, we ought to recognise that this same agenda would be an effective way of persuading those that do not strictly need to carry on working to do so, provided their jobs were more effectively tailored around their changing circumstances. And it is only by persuading all people to work longer, even those that do not need to for purely financial reasons, that we can hope to engineer the kind of cultural shift, or mitigate against the potential backlash, predicted above.

One way to think about this might be smoothing out the transition from work to retirement through a more structured phase of winding-down and gradual withdrawal. In the US there are already several initiatives by employees to encourage flexible retirement, such as Deloitte Consulting's Senior Leaders programme, which allows talented executives to redesign their work patterns to suit their circumstances so that they stay in the job rather than retire early.[103] As well as reducing their time commitment, the focus of senior employees' in this phase might shift towards preserving the value of their accumulated experience and knowledge so that it is not lost when they leave the organisation. One way this could be achieved would be through mentoring schemes.

Other problems

The idea that simply raising the state pension age will provide a solution to our predicament is symptomatic of the mechanistic tone of much of the political debate: it assumes (quite wrongly in our view) that very complex human behaviours and motivations can be manipulated from the centre, to meet objectives determined by the centre, without generating a whole series of unintended and often undesirable consequences.

One of the most obvious relates to the supply of informal care. As we argue in chapter 6, a key trend in the changing pattern of family structures is the emergence of 'beanpole' families, in which the relationship between grandparents and grandchildren is increasingly important.[104] With the growth of dual earner households many grandparents currently support their working children by providing care for their grandchildren. When working mothers are living with the father of their child, 24 per cent of grandparents carry out daytime childcare. Grandparents are particularly called upon when parents are separated, with this daycare support rising to 44.5 per cent of grandparents in families where the parents are separated.[105] The *Financial Times* recently identified 'the rise of the supergran' as a trend that was creating a 'three-generational win–win–win situation' for children, parents and grandparents alike.[106] But at the same time there is evidence that grandparents are increasingly reluctant to take on the burden of caring for grandchildren:

> What is arguably new therefore is not so much the pressure on grannies to do the childcare as their resistance to it. The revolutionary generation of women who challenged and adapted convention as they passed through earlier life-stages are perhaps in revolt against the traditional expectation of daughters – which they exercised themselves as daughters – for family childcare support. And this would help to explain our finding that, at a time when grandparents publicly claim to be providing more help than previous generations, many do not seem to be doing much at all.[107]

The same study, the most in-depth ever conducted into grandparenting, discovered that:

- the happiest grannies are those who achieved a balance of caring and part-time work: 87 per cent agree strongly that their role is rewarding, compared with 66 per cent of those working full time and 65 per cent of those not working
- of working grandmothers, the happiest are those being asked to do some caring (grandparenting only infrequently) while the unhappiest are those 'supergrans' being asked to juggle work with a lot of caring (grandparenting day and evenings at least several times a month).

It seems we cannot ask grandparents to work longer and to maintain their current levels of commitment to the upbringing of their grandchildren without risking serious consequences for their willingness to juggle both responsibilities and, at a deeper level, their unhappiness at being expected to.

Work and self-fulfilment

Understanding what ageing means for work requires that we look beyond the 'hard' issues of economics, labour markets and dependency ratios to the softer but arguably more promising cultural and attitudinal processes that could transform the way we think about employment and retirement, and about the relationship between the two. In particular, it means recognising that work is not just something that puts food on the table but something that can contribute to our sense of identity, happiness and fulfilment. From this viewpoint, the focus for reform should be qualitative as much as quantitative since the two are clearly related: it is not just how much or how long people work that matters, but the kind of work that they do and how it is organised.

In the future, as now, there will be many for whom a round-the-world 'holiday of a lifetime' is the ultimate source of fulfilment. But for many others, later life will also present an opportunity to realise long-held vocational aspirations. Retirement could become a very liberating space, a chance to 'dabble', to do the job one had always wanted to do but never had the chance. Self-employment among older people has increased significantly in the last two decades and may rise even further in the near future. The proportion of self-employed among the 60–64 age group has more than doubled in the last 25 years from 5 per cent in 1978 to 12 per cent in 1999.[108] With 50.5 per cent of baby boomers claiming they would 'rather be a self-employed entrepreneur than a 9–5 employee'[109] we might see an unprecedented rise in older people wanting to use the time and resources afforded by their retirement to start their own company.

An alternative agenda

An alternative, more holistic, agenda for redefining retirement would have the following key features. First, it would abandon the preservation of the 20/40/10 conception of working life as a guide to policy formation, and move towards a much more positive agenda of maximising the flexibility and choice open to people about how they define and pursue quality of life. Second, it would take as its aim to support all older people in developing new ways to combine economic and social activity to fit their circumstances, rather than focusing so narrowly on giving lower-income baby boomers the Hobson's choice of working longer or drawing an inadequate pension. Third, it would recognise that simply leaving individuals to address this problem, and extending choice and flexibility in what retirement means only to a privileged few, is a missed opportunity to harness these individual choices to the collective end of fundamentally reshaping the range of possibilities open to individuals about what retirement means.

In short, we need to redefine retirement: to envision a future in which periods of learning, caring, leisure and work occur at less discrete and less predictable points in the life cycle, and where the key challenge for public policy is to maximise the choices available to individuals (whatever their age) in terms of how they structure, prioritise and personalise these activities to suit their circumstances and preferences, and to foster the legitimacy and social expectations needed to make this possible. See figure 4.1 for a comparison of the old paradigm compared with the new.

One idea or motif that helps to capture the kinds of changes that this new agenda might imply is that of 'elderpreneurship'. Rather than viewing older people as largely passive dependants within large-scale systems of provision, we should view them as elderpreneurs who seek to create value for themselves and others by exploiting capital – be it

Figure 4.1 The old paradigm compared with the new

Old paradigm	New paradigm
Individual problem	Collective problem
Prolonging work	Redefining retirement
Must work	Want to work
Quantity of work	Quality of work
9–5 job	Elderpreneurship

financial, human, social or cultural[110] – to satisfy unmet needs.[111] A political agenda for supporting elderpreneurship might include the following elements.

Creating a country-wide network of micro-credit and venture capital funds aimed at older people

The contribution that small enterprises can make to job creation and social inclusion, particularly in deprived areas, is now well understood. There is also a growing interest in forms of social investment and social enterprise – for profit, but with a sense of social purpose or mission – as a means of promoting community regeneration. Another policy innovation, this time imported from the developing world, is that of micro-credit, a specialised financial product comprising small loans tailored to the needs of very small businesses, which seeks to evolve with them as they grow. The importance of these developments was reflected in the establishment of the Social Investment Task Force.[112] After the Task Force's report *Enterprising Communities* was published a community development venture fund, Bridges Community Ventures, was established backed by £40 million of public and private capital to provide equity to businesses in deprived areas.[113] A Community Development Finance Association has also been set up[114] and a number of local authorities have developed social enterprise strategies.[115] The government has also recently consulted on the part that a new legal structure, the 'community interest company', might play in facilitating these developments.[116]

We would seek to build on and extend this growing infrastructure to support and encourage older people interested in setting up a commercial or social enterprise. In the same way that the Prince's Trust[117] targets young people thinking of setting up a business, providing low-interest loans, grants, advice and support, a network of similar organisations should be set up for older people. One relatively small-scale example of what this might look like is provided by the charity Prime, a subsidiary of Age Concern, which is dedicated to giving those aged 50 and over the option, opportunity and support to become self-employed. Its main strands of work include: leading a national campaign to promote and support employment of those in this age group; working with an expanding network of partners to inform and support those in this age group in becoming self-employed; and developing research and knowledge into self-employment for those in this age group. Combining the advice and support provided by an organisation like Prime with financial backing through local venture capital and micro-credit would provide a potent combination for harnessing older people's talents and energies.

Underwriting risk through an Elder Credit Guarantee Scheme

Although baby boomers may have a larger pool of financial assets on which to draw when they retire, they will understandably be more risk averse than other groups. To overcome this risk aversion when it comes to using assets to finance entrepreneurial activities, an Elder Credit Guarantee Scheme could be established. Just as the Export Credits Guarantee Department mitigates some of the risk to British firms operating abroad, elder credit guarantees would allow older people to use a portion of their pension, savings or home equity secure in the knowledge that at least some of it was underwritten either by the state or through some form of public–private partnership. The scheme could be administered by the Small Business Service and dovetail with existing schemes such as the Small Firms Loan Guarantee scheme, which guarantees loans from approved lenders to small firms with viable business plans who lack the security to borrow money independently.[118]

Establishing wisdom banks

Organisations like Experience Corps and TimeBank have already established the principle that social participation of various kinds can be facilitated and enhanced through the creation of local institutions to act as brokers and intermediaries. To this end, we propose the establishment of 'wisdom banks'. These would combine:

- the employment brokering services offered by public institutions like the Employment Service and the Experience Corps, and private organisations like temping and recruitment agencies, in order proactively to map local needs and skills gaps in the private and voluntary sectors, and match these to the skills and experience of local older people
- new forms of human capital development and banking,[119] wisdom banks would provide local, community-based institutions for accrediting knowledge and learning, particularly that gained in informal settings, as well as a learning brokerage service, helping individuals to identify and pursue new learning opportunities. This ties in to the discussion of 'Communiversities' in chapter 5.

In this way, it might be possible to re-create and validate a twenty-first-century notion of the 'community elder'.

Tackling age discrimination through cultural change

As we saw in chapter 2, the government is preparing legislation to tackle age discrimination in line with the European employment directive.[120] Experience with the Age Discrimination in Employment Act in the US suggests that anti-discrimination legislation is a crucial foundation for change, but by itself does not solve the problem. Getting to the root of the problem requires a deeper cultural shift, for which formal legal instruments are a necessary but not sufficient condition. Alongside, this 'hard' power, there are a number of 'softer' strategies that might be employed. For example:

- *Encouraging forms of flexible retirement and 'winding-down phases'* During this time employers and employees would work to rebalance the types and patterns of work they are doing to fit their changing circumstances. Government could model this approach in the public sector.

- *Integrating recruitment and retirement* Employers and employees should put as much emphasis on retirement (exit) strategies as they do on their recruitment (entry) strategies, to ensure better succession planning and that the value of employees – particularly the tacit knowledge they have accumulated in the course of their career – is not lost when they retire. There would be considerable scope for retirement and recruitment to be much more closely integrated through, for example, mentoring programmes that provided an opportunity for the newly recruited employee to benefit from the knowledge and experience of the retiring employee.

Fostering innovation for new kinds of financial services products

As Andrew Dilnot has argued,[121] one of the reasons for the perceived crisis in pension provision is the lack of alternative savings products and vehicles that may be better attuned to the current needs and circumstances of the baby boom generation. Too many assets, and especially property, are seen as something you build up but do not run down. Yet the potential for this to mitigate some of the current problems is illustrated by the market for equity release products – which allow homeowners to unlock some of the value of their homes, and is particularly important given levels of home ownership among the baby boomers. Levels of product innovation and consumer take-up within this market have grown very rapidly in recent years from £44 million annual sales in 1996 to £852 million in 2002. Between 2001 and 2002 alone the market grew by 49 per cent.[122] The government should work closely with the Financial Services Authority and financial services firms to ensure that the fiscal and regulatory landscape is attuned to encouraging this kind of innovation. And, as a society, we may need to get used to thinking differently about how assets are built up, used and passed on. We consider this subject in more detail in chapter 6.

To sum up:

- Work is crucial to the way we think about the ageing society. For many, the central challenge it presents is the welfare demands imposed by one generation on the next, hence the discussion of a 'pensions time bomb'.
- Current responses have tended to treat the problem as an individual rather than social matter, and to concentrate on preserving the outdated 20/40/10 paradigm of working life.
- Not only does this narrow the range of policy instruments available in the long run; it also increases the likelihood of causing resentment and animosity among baby boomers forced to work longer.
- An alternative strategy would be to focus on transforming that paradigm by focusing on the potential role for older people as 'elderpreneurs', creating value by using different kinds of financial, human, cultural and social capital to satisfy their and others' needs. The kinds of policy initiatives that might facilitate this include:
  - creating a country-wide network of local *micro-credit* and *venture capital funds* targeted at older people
  - introducing a government-backed risk-underwriting scheme for new start-ups (an *elder credits guarantee scheme*)
  - establishing local *wisdom banks*
  - tackling age discrimination through *cultural change*
  - fostering innovation in new, more flexible *savings and financial services products*.

5. Communities and environments

'Providing for old age' is a familiar refrain, but the really important question is 'providing what?'. Within the terms of the current debate, the answer is clear. On the one hand, providing for old age means that individuals are responsible for providing financial security, accumulating the assets and savings needed to provide an income in later life over and above a minimal level of state provision. On the other hand, providing for old age means putting in place the systems for providing and financing care for older people as they become more dependent on others for the performance of everyday tasks and routines.

These are important and very challenging issues, as widespread concerns about the savings gap and the capacity of the residential and nursing care sector testify. But the conception of the good life that underpins them is very narrow. They are deficit models, which exclude many aspects of what people see as good lives. As such, they are necessary but not sufficient foundations on which to build a comprehensive understanding of providing for old age. For the policy agenda to be meaningful it must be concerned with all the conditions necessary for the pursuit of a good later life, not simply those that have traditionally fallen under the auspices of the welfare state.

In particular, this agenda needs to emphasise not just individual needs and activities and financial capital, but also to recognise the importance of social needs, social activities and social capital. Our priority should be to understand how we can create good lives through participation. In this chapter, we address the question of how to develop a new framework that recognises the social underpinnings of good older lives.

Social capital and the challenge of participation

The reason why participation is so crucial is clear from the literature on social capital as well as what we know about the baby boomers. The concept of 'social capital' – defined as 'features of social organisation, such as civic participation, norms of reciprocity and trust in others, that facilitate cooperation for mutual benefit'[123] – has acquired an increasingly pivotal place in contemporary policy-making debates. This is rooted in a growing consensus on the positive correlation between social capital and a range of beneficial social outcomes, including economic growth, higher educational attainment, lower levels of crime and better health.[124]

More recently, scholars have sought to draw a distinction between three different types of social capital:

- *bonding* social capital, characterised by strong bonds (or 'social glue'), for instance among family members or among members of an ethnic group
- *bridging* social capital, characterised by weaker, less dense but more cross-cutting ties (or 'social oil'), for instance with business associates, acquaintances, friends from different ethnic groups and friends of friends
- *linking* social capital, characterised by connections between those with differing levels of power or social status, eg links between the political elite and the general public or between individuals from different social classes.[125]

Social capital has already come to occupy a more prominent place in the ageing policy debate. In particular, the value of volunteering as a lever for building social capital has been taken up by government enthusiastically. In *Winning the Generation Game*, the Cabinet Office Performance and Innovation Unit (now the Strategy Unit) called for the government to help 'older people to make use of their skills and experience for the benefit of the wider community'.[126] Following this analysis, a new organisation was created in 2002 to encourage and facilitate volunteering by those aged 50 and over. Experience Corps was set up as an independent, non-profit-making company, funded by a grant-in-aid from the Home Office.[127] It acts as a broker, seeking to match the skills and experience of older people to the identified needs of individuals and organisations in the community.

But, while Experience Corps represents a step in the right direction, not least as a way of trying to generate a more positive conception of ageing, it is not clear that the need to increase participation is yet understood to be a pressing policy challenge in itself. Yet you need not look very far to see why it ought to be. First, studies suggest that individuals who are socially isolated are at two to five times greater risk of dying from all causes than if they are not isolated in this way.[128] Second, because of changing patterns of family structure and the prevalence of divorce and separation among the baby boomer generation (which we study in more detail in chapter 6 but which was considered in the discussion of the baby boomers' liberalism in chapter 3), members of this age group are likely to have lower levels of 'bonding' social capital. Between 40 and 50 per cent of baby boomers are likely to be 'living solo' by the age of 75,[129] with clear implications for the provision of informal care and support for routine activities as well as overall well-being: 'Social capital, particularly bonding social capital provided by family and close friends, provides tangible assistance and care and also creates a sense of well being and belonging whereas its absence leads to isolation and depression.'[130]

Third, the evidence seems to suggest that the baby boomers are a disconnected generation in a wider sense, more detached from their local communities than earlier generations and, though the data does not allow us to be certain, therefore having lower levels of 'bridging' social capital than other generations:

- *They claim to belong to fewer social networks than either older or younger generations* Only 33.5 per cent of baby boomers agree that they 'are part of several networks of people who communicate and do things together', compared with 39 per cent of the older and 51.5 per cent of the younger generations.[131]
- *The social attachments they do have are likely to be less meaningful* Only 42 per cent of baby boomers agreed with the statement that 'the groups and organisations I belong to mean a lot to me', compared with 54 per cent and 52.5 per cent among the older and younger generations respectively.[132]
- *They are less interested in and feel less of a sense of belonging to their neighbourhoods* On the MORI Social Values indices, which cluster a basket of responses to related questions, the baby boomers are correlated much more weakly with 'neighbourhood focus' (meaning a 'strong interest in local events and one's neighbours generating important feeling of belonging') than older generations.[133]
- *They feel more like outsiders* On the set of trends associated with being an 'underdog' ('the feeling of not belonging to the local community and not being integrated into wider society'), the baby boomers identify much more strongly with this than older generations do.[134]
- *They are much less attached to their geographical communities than previous generations* 44 per cent of baby boomers claim that they would emigrate if they had the chance, almost two and a half times as many as the over-55 generation with this view.[135]
- *They are less eager than older generations to participate in voluntary work* While 39 per cent of the over-55 age group supported the statement that 'everyone has a duty to do voluntary work at some time in their lives', only 26.5 per cent of baby boomers agreed.[136]

This has potentially important policy implications since, as Wenger argues, 'in the years after retirement, the roles of social networks become increasingly important in providing access to support in the face of escalating losses and growing frailty.'[137]

Quality of life through participation

So if we want to move towards a more rounded conception of the good later life, one that acknowledges the importance of participation and social activity alongside more individual forms of security, what are the forums or arenas that matter most or seem the most promising for building new bonds?

Housing and neighbourhood design

An obvious place to start is with the built environment. As Christopher Alexander wrote more than 25 years ago, 'Clearly, old people cannot be integrated socially as in traditional cultures unless they are first integrated physically – unless they share the same streets, shops, services, and common land with everyone else.'[138] Similarly, many people are forced to go into residential care not because they are unable to look after themselves but because they are disabled by a physical infrastructure (in terms of housing stock) and a human infrastructure (in terms of homecare provision) that are inappropriately designed for their needs.

Alexander's solution in *A Pattern Language* is a particular kind of neighbourhood planning to promote the full integration and participation of older people in their community. This is based on concentric rings, with a large group house at the core where cooking and nursing care are provided, a series of smaller cottages nearby, with additional cottages further out mixed in among other houses in the neighbourhood, but never more than 200 yards from the core.[139] The rationale is essentially that the neighbourhood can co-evolve with an older person as that person's needs change.

This is a distinctly different approach from current practice, which often either presents older people with a Hobson's choice between staying in a house that no longer suits them or moving into residential care, or encourages the creation of 'grey ghettos' – whole towns marketed on a preponderance of two-bedroom houses and a claim to provide refuge from the pressures and dangers of urban living. Neither form of segregation reflects particularly well on our capacity as a society to manage intergenerational relations.

One need not agree with Alexander's particular prescription to see that the notion of neighbourhoods that learn or co-evolve is very attractive. Interestingly, it is a lesson that seems to underpin a government programme, which made £100 million available to local authorities over three years to enable them to develop preventative strategies for adult services, in partnership with other agencies. In the Netherlands, the development of home zones, originally envisaged as little more than a traffic calming measure, has unexpectedly led to major increases in social capital because it changed the way people in the area interacted with their public space.[140]

Technology also opens up the potential for older people to live independently in their own home for longer. The concept of the 'smart home' equipped with all sorts of technological wizardry from motorised cupboards, which can be lowered or raised to motion detectors that light the way to the bathroom at night, is familiar from the many visions of the 'home of the future' distilled over the last half-century. What lies more immediately within reach is the potential to perform online many of the routine caring or supervisory activities that would otherwise require residential care. Technology can never be a substitute for people, but both Germany and Spain have experimented with broadband projects that provide online home care or 'televisits' from medical practitioners.[141]

Intergenerational understanding and bridging social capital

As a recent Demos pamphlet argued, older generations are not the only group whose ties to community have been severed: the bonds between the community and the children growing up within it have also been severed, resulting in a decline in the collective sense of responsibility that a community feels for other people's children and the increasing privatisation of parenting.[142]

A number of initiatives have shown how these problems can be overcome through a concerted effort to foster intergenerational understanding, and to build bridges between the generations. *Ein Schritt ins Alter* ('A step into age') is a joint public–private supported and funded Austrian project that promotes intergenerational understanding. The project tries to help primary school children appreciate the disabilities that older people have to cope with in an everyday context. The children are made to wear glasses that cloud their vision, gloves that make it difficult to grasp things, and weights that make it harder to move their legs. After experiencing these disabilities, the children discuss ideas about how the everyday environment and products can be designed for all ages. Plans are afoot to extend the project to adults as well. Age Concern Northern Ireland has set up several projects bringing together older and younger people to undertake shared activities, from environmental initiatives to glass painting. Big Brothers Big Sisters of America is a youth service organisation that matches adults with children for weekly shared activities.[143] In 1998 Big Brothers Big Sisters International was created to encourage and support the creation of similar mentoring schemes around the world, including the UK.[144]

The workplace

Workplaces are important to sustain older people's participation in the wider community in two respects. For older people who want to carry on working beyond state pension age (as the government hopes) but who have a fairly substantial caring responsibility for a spouse or partner, reconciling these two imperatives will require the development of an 'eldercare' infrastructure. Employers are in a strong position to facilitate this, not least because there will be overlaps with (and perhaps even economies of scale from) the provision of childcare, which is seen as an increasingly important aspect of 'family-friendly' employment practices. Where the primary caring responsibility is discharged by the children of older people, 'elder-enabled' workplaces would be one way of offsetting demand for residential care, since employees would not be prevented from continuing to care for a parent or older relative by being in work.

A good example of this principle is the charity BEN, a motor and allied trades benevolent fund, which joined forces with Peugeot to set up an elder day care centre at its plant in Coventry in 1997. Since it opened the centre, dubbed the 'granny crèche' by the press, has provided care for around 25 members a day.[145]

Health and fitness

In the US, preventative health initiatives have sought to combine the personal opportunity to get fit with the social opportunity of meeting new people. What is striking about this in terms of community participation is that it is indirect: building social capital is not the object of the exercise (although it is clearly one of the main incentives for those taking part), but rather a desirable by-product of a scheme primarily aimed at individual well-being. For example, the AARP (formerly American Association of Retired Persons) is piloting a project in two cities designed to encourage older people to exercise by emphasising the fun and social aspects of physical activity. The project works on a number of fronts, including: providing targeted information about the benefits of exercise; developing a directory of local opportunities to take part in; acting at the local community level to remove barriers to daily exercise; and setting up new opportunities to get involved in shared activities, including walking clubs and special triathlons.[146]

Schools and learning

Learning will be a much more important component of people's later lives in the future than it was for earlier generations. More than two-thirds – 69 per cent – of baby boomers are interested in undertaking learning activities in the future, more than double the figure for the 55 and over age group. Interestingly, the baby boomers are significantly more interested in learning from home or at a college or university than in the workplace.[147] There are a number of possible explanations:

- a growing emphasis on 'lifelong learning', and the emergence of an infrastructure (including institutions such as LearnDirect and the University of the Third Age) to support it
- the educational attainment of this generation compared with earlier generations, and the greater confidence that this generates in their capacity to learn[148]
- a desire to remain active and intellectually challenged after leaving full-time work
- higher levels of technological and particularly online literacy, which matters because of the importance of information and communication technology platforms in the delivery of distance learning; 55 per cent of baby boomers use the internet but only 9 per cent of those aged 65 and over do[149]
- the rise of 'active citizenship' and 'co-production' – the idea that long-term improvements in the quality of public goods such as education and health cannot be delivered on behalf of citizens, but instead depend on their active involvement.[150] Access to growing volumes of information is a crucial aspect of this. In the US, for example, the National Council on the Aging (NCOA) provides an online benefit calculator, www.benefitscheckup.org, which enables older adults to find out whether they are claiming all the benefits to which they are entitled.[151] Similarly, the AARP offers online health information and expert advice through a dedicated 'Health and Wellness' section on its website.[152] But while the provision of information may increase the capacity for, say, patients to take preventative action before a health problem develops too far, it also places a premium on being able to manage, evaluate and apply information from alternative sources that are of variable quality and reliability.

This represents an important opportunity for universities and other learning providers, particularly in the development of online content and distance learning. But even at the very local level, we might see a shift towards the '24-hour school', with local education providers or voluntary organisations providing learning opportunities, either as a way of subsiding their main activities or as a way of building community cohesion. In the United States, older people's eagerness to learn for leisure is being harnessed by the not-for-profit organisation Elderhostel. Founded in 1975, Elderhostel combines education and travel through a range of learning programmes for the over-55 age group in locations across the globe.[153] Similarly, Learning Annex is an alternative adult education organisation in the US and Canada offering short, inexpensive courses on issues ranging from health and healing to high technology.[154] In the UK, the Department for Education and Skills is promoting the concept of the 'extended school': 'schools which act as a focal point for a range of family, community and health services for their students, families, staff and the wider population'.[155] Some of these schools attract 1,000 community learners a week, and provide a base for all kinds of community-based organisation (including those providing services to older people) that would otherwise be homeless. They also represent another way of building bridges between young and old. As the evaluation of one such school concluded:

> What it did in reducing that distance between the old and the young was phenomenal because the young suddenly realised that the older people have a wealth of experience. And the older people began to realise that kids are human; they are not threatening just because they are in groups.[156]

The Community Action Network is helping to promote the concept of the 'communiversity': a community of local people who come together to pool their capacity – resources and skills – and to draw on the capacity of others to address their needs. This builds on a highly successful model developed in Craigmillar, Scotland, which has succeeded in getting its learning provision accredited by Napier University.[157]

Parks and green spaces

Parks and green spaces are crucial social assets that can fulfil many complex urban needs, promoting social inclusion and providing a sense of place and community.[158] They provide opportunities and facilities for many of the everyday activities and experiences that are so important to quality of life and participation, whether it is walking a dog, playing sport or providing a safe place for children to play. But as research by Demos and Comedia in the mid-1990s showed, many parks and open spaces are in decline, and older groups are often reluctant to take full advantage of them because of concerns about their safety.[159]

However, older people can play a role in reviving green spaces by providing the active management, involvement and sense of shared ownership that is often crucial to their success and sustainability. In Italy people living in an old people's centre took over responsibility for a park in decline and transformed it into a hotbed of diverse cultural activity for the whole community, with card tables, open-air performances, a jogging track, cycle paths and gardens.[160]

Diversity

Cultural and ethnic diversity is set to be one of the distinguishing features of the baby boom generation compared with earlier generations of older people.[161] This places an additional premium on promoting participation and social inclusion, as older people from ethnic minority communities often suffer disproportionately from poor provision of health, social care and housing, as the Royal Commission on Long Term Care for the Elderly noted:

> All providers of services should be culturally sensitive while meeting the diverse needs of their communities, and this is especially relevant in areas when black and ethnic minority elders

> are few in number. *There can be no doubt that a greater sense of community and fostering of trust between different communities will only come if services develop in this way* [emphasis added].[162]

The Commission praised the performance of the community and voluntary sector in 'incorporating a rich cultural component to their services' in these areas.[163] The unique contribution that community-based organisations can make in building trust and social inclusion more effectively than traditional forms of statutory provision was acknowledged in a recent Demos report.[164]

There is a challenge here for organisations that represent or lobby on behalf of older people. In the US, the AARP tailors its services to the growing Hispanic population in the country, not only offering a Spanish version of its website, but also a separate Spanish magazine for those aged over 50 called *Segunda Juventud* ('The Second Youth').[165]

Political activism

We have already seen that baby boomers have a distinguished track record of political activism and protest, and have to some extent defined themselves by a marked lack of deference to, respect for and trust in formal authority, and a willingness to eschew formal channels of political communication in favour of direct action of various kinds.

1960s	Aldermaston March and anti-apartheid demonstrations
1970s	women's movement, pro-abortion marches; attempted to unionise a major publishing company, but failed
1980s	more feminist activities, marching against Corrie, Benyon and White amendments to abortion legislation; anti-nuclear campaign, arrested in demonstrations at Greenham Common Air Force Base

	and again at Dungeness Nuclear Power Station; support for miners' strike; sit-down protest against attack on Libya
1990s	march against Gulf War; march for Stephen Lawrence campaign
2000s	demonstrating against war in Afghanistan and Iraq; support for firefighters' strike.

Female baby boomer aged 56 outlines her activist 'CV'

These characteristics of the baby boom generation still seem to hold true:

- Baby boomers remain the least deferential generation. Only 14 per cent of baby boomers believe that 'in general, the people in charge know best', compared with 26 per cent of the older generation and 20 per cent of the younger.[166]
- 46.5 per cent of baby boomers believe 'that strikes and demonstrations are signs of a healthy social system', compared with only 37 per cent of younger generations and 35 per cent of the older generation.[167]
- Baby boomers are more likely to have signed an environmental petition than any other generation.[168]
- Baby boomers are more likely to have participated in a boycott of a company's products on ethical grounds than any other generation.[169]
- Baby boomers are less interested in formal politics than older generations,[170] a pattern reflected in their electoral participation. Around 62 per cent of baby boomers voted in the 2001 General Election compared with 70 per cent of the older generation.[171]
- Baby boomers distrust politicians more than other generations: asked if politicians are honest, 68 per cent disagree; this compares with 61.5 per cent of the older generation and 62.5 of the younger.[172]

These attributes may have important implications for how we should expect baby boomers to relate to local political institutions in the future. Instead of populating the benches of parish or city councils, perhaps the baby boomers will continue to get more fulfilment from participating in direct action of various kinds. The anti-war march held in London on 15 February 2003 showed that younger generations had no monopoly on large-scale, street protest.

In Denmark, older people have already begun to get involved in more activist forms of political participation. In the early 1990s, a new grassroots movement of older people was established called the C Team. As Walker explains, the group 'is independent of established organisations representing older people as well as political parties; it arranges mass demonstrations and other actions aimed at preventing cuts in health and social services and improving provisions for frail older people'.[173]

Online technologies

Baby boomers are almost as keen on ICTs as younger generations are. For example, 85 per cent of baby boomers own mobile phones, compared with only 37 per cent of the over-65 age group. 62 per cent of baby boomers use the internet, compared with only 13 per cent of the over-65 age group.[174] And two-thirds of baby boomers think that 'computers and other modern electronic devices are good fun', compared with just one-third of older generations.[175]

Coupled with the development of high-speed internet connections, this ICT literacy could have several important ramifications for reducing isolation, by enabling the development of new, more diverse 'virtual' communities. In the US, the AARP hosts a dedicated 'online community' on its website; in the UK Age Concern has set up a 'baby boomer bistro'.[176] Both services offer older people the opportunity to build friendships and exchange ideas and experiences via the internet.

Investing in participation

What this analysis suggests is that, alongside long-term savings products and provision for long-term care, there are a whole range of other aspects of good later lives in which we ought collectively to 'invest', from community-based organisations to learning centres to community health initiatives to eldercare in the workplace. And the real kicker is that by investing in participation in this way, we may be able to offset the costs of providing for old age in a narrower, financial sense. Healthier, fitter older people will impose less of a burden on the NHS. The more individuals are able to stay in their own homes for longer, the less it will cost to provide residential care places.

But if we do not invest in these kinds of social and community institutions and practices today, then in 15 or 20 years' time when their value is more fully understood it will be too late to create them, and their long-term benefits will have been squandered. Government, and the networks of agencies through which it operates, must take a long view and understand that these short-term investments will pay dividends in terms of lower bills later. The central question is: how do we create a political strategy that encourages and motivates the key, strategic public sector institutions to understand the value of investing in social and cultural capital through the kinds of approaches outlined here, and that makes it politically attractive enough for them to do so?

So which institutions ought to be responsible? If the aim is to lower costs to the Exchequer in the long run then perhaps it should be the Treasury. If the aim is to ease the financial and operational pressures on core services and to diversify provision perhaps it should be the spending departments. If the aim is to tailor needs around local circumstances then perhaps local authorities should be given the resources and authorisation to make this happen. Whichever institution or combination of institutions is given the incentive or the duty for developing this agenda, the task of fostering these kinds of activities on the ground can and should be distributed through local networks, which are in a better position to coordinate activities around local needs than any one agency acting in isolation. Putting in place the systems for sharing knowledge and practice laterally from one location to another will then become crucial if this approach is to reach sufficient scale and engineer the kind of transformation that it promises to make possible.

To sum up:

- Providing for old age is usually understood in terms of financial security, but this ignores the many other aspects of what people see as good lives.
- In particular, we need to emphasise not just individual needs and financial capital but social needs and social capital.
- The value of social networks and participation is increasingly recognised and has begun to be incorporated into policy, but the scale of the challenge is not well understood.
- The baby boomers have lower levels of 'bonding' social capital because of higher levels of divorce and separation, with serious implications for the provision of care and support.
- They also seem to have lower levels of 'bridging' social capital, belonging to fewer social networks and feeling more disconnected from the wider community.
- This suggests that alongside long-term savings products and provision of care, there is a wide range of other aspects of good later lives in which we ought collectively to invest, such as:
  - housing and neighbourhood design
  - intergenerational understanding
  - the workplace
  - health and fitness
  - schools and learning
  - parks and green spaces
  - diversity
  - political activism
  - online technologies.
- Investing in these kinds of institutions and practices could also offset some of the costs of providing for old age in a

narrower, financial sense; for instance healthier, fitter older people will impose less of a burden on the NHS. Important questions therefore remain about who should be responsible for motivating and coordinating this investment.

6. Intergenerational equity

Sometimes I fantasise thinking that I would like to live in a hotel. I would like the ability to not be dependent. I would like the economic freedom to choose. On the other hand I would find that a very lonely and horrible prospect if actually I wanted a lot of care and help from my family.

Female baby boomer

So far, we have looked at how new social practices and institutional reform could make life for older people more attractive and more sustainable. We have examined baby boomers' priorities for personal fulfilment, and particularly the part that work might play, as well as the ways in which their quality of life will be shaped through social participation of various kinds.

An underlying premise of this analysis has been that, in the long run, radically better outcomes will only arise by changing personal behaviour and transforming social expectations. In other words, new and innovative solutions to managing the transition to an ageing society will only really be possible if they can be legitimised.

But in reality there is a deeper set of issues that needs to be addressed. For possibilities for redefining later life depend on more fundamental questions about the distribution of wealth and responsibility between generations. Working and saving generates a very visible form of this contract between the generations. But of course, the pre-eminent bond between one generation and the next is not created through the social security system but through the family. Our sense of obligation to other generations within society as a whole is inextricably tied up in our sense of obligation to other generations within our family. In this sense, families are the glue that sticks generations together. It is in the family that the dependencies of one generation on another, and the changing patterns of this dependency over time, are felt most acutely. Families are also informal but highly effective marketplaces or clearing houses for managing the transfer of all kinds of resources from one generation to the next. Parents bring up their children. Grandparents babysit their grandchildren. Inheritances are passed down from the older generation to younger generations. Children care for their parents in their old age.

For these and many other reasons families must be central to the task of adapting to an ageing society. Yet surprisingly little attention has actually been paid, at least within the mainstream debate, to the impact that our ageing society will have on the norms and rhythms of family life, and to the informal processes, activities and flows of resources that structure relations between the generations. In this chapter, we outline three issues that we believe are worthy of further exploration.

We address how the baby boomers might become engaged in the renegotiation of a much wider welfare settlement, involving both the structure of the prominence of different forms of taxation, state-driven redistribution and public investment as well as the transfer of private wealth and opportunity between generations through families.

The historical settlement

As we saw in chapter 2, a growing older population is seen to threaten the historical compact underpinning the postwar welfare state. That is because the major welfare systems, such as pensions, health and long-term care, have largely been organised on a 'pay-as-you-go' basis whereby the current adult population finances the needs of current older people, in expectation of the same treatment when their time comes. The pensioner support (old-age dependency) ratio, which calculates the number of people aged 15–64 relative to the number of older people above 65 needing to be supported, therefore deteriorates. In 2000, there were 3.4 people aged 15–64 for every person above state pension age. By 2040, this figure will have fallen to 2.4.[177]

This settlement is already unravelling. As was suggested in chapter 2, the UK is in a better fiscal position than many other countries to deal with this, for several reasons:

- The demographic transition is on a smaller scale than that facing many other countries (see table 6.1).
- The state pension system has been radically scaled back in recent decades. Since 1980, the basic state pension has only been uprated in line with inflation. Because earnings tend to rise faster than prices, the cumulative effect of this change has been to reduce drastically the value of the pension relative to average incomes:
  - In 1979, the basic state pension was 23 per cent of average male earnings.
  - By 2000, this had fallen to 15 per cent.
  - By 2040, it is expected to drop to just 8 per cent.[178]
- As a result, the cost of the basic state pension as a proportion of GDP is actually expected to fall over the next 40 years, from 3.7 per cent in 2000 to 3.2 per cent in 2040.[179]
- Personal pension provision has been radically extended. In 1998, it was estimated that around 56 per cent of employees were in personal or occupational pension schemes of some kind, with another 20 per cent belonging to SERPS (the state earnings-related pensions scheme) and a further 21 per cent not covered at all.[180]
- Expectations of collective welfare provision have diminished. In 1998, the government pledged to invert the 60/40 split between state contributions and private pensions in current pensioner incomes.[181]

Table 6.1 Population aged 65 and over as a percentage of those aged 15–64, in selected countries

	1975	2000	2025	2050
EU member states				
UK	22.6[a]	24.4	32.8	39.2
France	21.5	24.5	36.2	46.7
Germany	23.3	24.1	39.0	54.7
Italy	18.9	26.7	40.6	68.1
Spain	16.1	24.8	36.1	73.8
Weighted average of all EU member states	20.7	24.5	37.1	54.7
Other countries				
Japan	11.6	25.2	49.0	71.3
Canada	12.9	18.5	32.6	40.9
US	16.3	18.6	29.3	34.9

[a]Figure for 1976
Sources: United Nations, *World Population Ageing 1950–2050*, 2001; Government Actuary's Department historical data and 2001-based interim principal population projections cited in GAD, *Simplicity, Security and Choice*

But while the sense of collective threat may have been assuaged by the increasing individualisation of the responsibility for providing financial security, we can expect some shortfall for some people, the oft-forgotten poor and economically inactive baby boomers, in the finances available for retirement. This leads to a deeper question about how we determine the priorities for future investment and about the political strength of different interest groups in shaping them.

One presumption is that baby boomers will need to use up more of their own assets in the last stages of life. As suggested in chapter 4, historically there has been a cultural tendency to view pensions as the only asset that you build up in order to run down when needed.

Other assets, including property, have been seen as a nest egg to accumulate and then pass on. But as concerns about financial insecurity mount, the traditional expectations of inheritance may well be challenged. Consumer research indicates that 86 per cent of children whose parents would qualify for home equity release products would now be pleased for their parents if they spent their assets to support themselves in retirement rather than passing them on as inheritance. Nevertheless, the resilience of the cultural attachment to the idea of a nest egg is indicated by the fact that 73 per cent of children whose parents qualify for equity release products are still planning to leave their own children an inheritance.[182]

There is also much greater potential for direct dependence of older parents on their middle-aged children at a time when they are becoming more likely to have extended financial responsibilities for their own children through extended adolescence and the new costs of higher education, as well as a stronger presumption that they will have to provide a greater contribution to their own pension financing. The outcome of this conflict will depend partly on the stance of baby boomers towards other issues. The most powerful expression of this is through family. What do we know about this?

The changing family

Partnerships and family have changed massively in the last 50 years. A full survey of the underlying reasons for this change is beyond the scope of this pamphlet, but they include the elusive 'sexual revolution' of which the early baby boomers were the vanguard, a cultural shift in values and attitudes concerning marriage and children, changing conceptions of how the family unit fits in with other demands (particularly those imposed by the labour market), reform of divorce law, falling birth rates, and many others.

Although both baby boomer cohorts have been part of this radical transformation in patterns of family and partnership formation, the early and the late baby boomer generations have experienced the main parameters of this shift differently.[183]

Marriage and cohabitation

While the first baby boomer generation has among the highest marriage rates in this century, the second baby boomer cohort marks the beginning of a sustained decline in marriage rates at all ages – see tables 6.2 and 6.3.

Table 6.2 Percentage of women and men who had 'ever married' by age 30, by year of birth

Year of birth	Women	Men
1921	81.9	75.4
1926	84.9	77.6
1931	88.9	80.9
1936	90.6	82.7
1941	90.7	83.0
1946	91.7	82.9
1951	88.1	78.0
1956	83.6	72.0
1961	74.3	61.5
1966	65.0	49.8
1971	53.0	37.1

Source: Office for National Statistics, *Marriage, Divorce and Adoption Statistics, England and Wales* 2000

Table 6.3 Percentage of women who had 'never married' at selected ages for birth cohorts

Age	born 1916–20	born 1931–5	born 1946–50	born 1961–5
20	92	81	72	86
25	46	25	19	51
30	24	11	8	32

Source: Office for National Statistics, *Social Trends, England and Wales* 31, 2001

Table 6.4 Average (mean) age at first marriage during specific time periods

Period	Women	Men
1926–30	25.54	27.36
1936–40	25.38	27.51
1946–50	24.54	27.15
1956–60	23.49	25.90
1966–70	22.47	24.64
1976–80	22.89	25.19
1986–90	24.59	26.71
1996–2000	27.71	29.85

Source: Office for National Statistics, *Marriage, Divorce and Adoption Statistics, England and Wales* 2000

There is also a difference between early and late baby boomers in terms of the average age of marriage, as women and men from the later baby boomer cohort have remained single for longer. While the first baby boomer cohort married at an earlier average age than previous generations, the second baby boomer cohort again saw a rise in the average age at marriage – see table 6.4. Although this shift to fewer and later marriages among the second baby boomer cohort is partly offset by higher rates of cohabitation, more late baby boomers than previous generations remain single and outside any form of partnership. According to ONS projections quoted by Evandrou and Falkingham 'over 10 per cent of women and 16 per cent of men from the 1960s cohort [1961–5] will not have formed a marital union or be in a permanent cohabiting union by the time they reach age 50. This compares with 4 per cent of women and 8 per cent of men born in 1946.'[184]

Divorce and separation

Rising divorce and separation rates among early and late baby boomers have increased the propensity for both baby boomer cohorts to 'singleness' and living alone. This is expected to continue

Table 6.5 Percentage of women and men who had 'ever divorced' by age 35 by year of birth

Year of birth	Women	Men
1926	4.5	3.3
1931	4.4	3.5
1936	6.0	5.3
1941	10.7	9.7
1946	16.2	13.7
1951	18.3	16.6
1956	19.8	16.9
1961	19.3	15.7
1966	17.4	13

Source: Office for National Statistics, *Marriage, Divorce and Adoption Statistics, England and Wales* 2000

and these rates will be only partially offset by declining rates of widowhood owing to improvements in life expectancy. The number of divorces in Britain has risen continuously from 30,977 in 1962, to 124,911 in 1972, to 159,396 in 1982 and to 175,144 in 1992, after which there was a slight decline to 154,628 in 2000[185] – see table 6.5. Moreover, according to Evandrou and Falkingham it 'is forecast that 41 per cent of the 1940s cohort [1946–50] will be living alone by age 75 compared with 38 per cent of the 1930s cohort [1931–5] and 37 per cent of the 1916–20 cohort. Furthermore, a quarter (26 per cent) of the 1960s cohort will already be lone householders by age 60.' This makes it 'likely that close to half of the 1960s [1961–5] boomers will be living solo by age 75'.[186]

Remarriage and 'reconstituted families'

Accompanying the rise in divorce rates is an increase in remarriage and 'reconstituted families' among both baby boomer cohorts. The number of remarriages rose from 58,198 in 1962, to 70,776 in 1967, to 120,179 in 1972 and then continued to fluctuate between 120,000 and 140,000 for the remainder of the century. Rising remarriage in turn results in an increase of the occurrence of 'reconstituted families' and stepchildren. Nearly one in five of women born in 1956 have remarried at least once by the age of 45.[187] It has been estimated that of the children born to the second baby boomer generation around 6 per cent will have become stepchildren of a married couple and 7 per cent of a cohabiting couple.[188]

Lone parenthood

Rising divorce and separation rates also contribute to an increase in the occurrence of lone parenthood. In the period from 1974 to 1993 the 'incidence of lone motherhood at a given age increased dramatically between women born in 1946–50 and 1961–5: 12 per cent of women from the 1961–5 age group were lone mothers at age 30, compared with just 5 per cent of the 1946–50 cohort at the same age.' Moreover, the number of lone fathers more than doubled in that same time period.[189]

Later and fewer children

There is also a clear distinction in childbearing patterns between early and late baby boomers. While the first baby boomer generation tended to marry earlier and also have children earlier, the second baby boomer generation married and had children later. The average age of the mother at childbirth increased from 26.2 in 1971, to 26.9 in 1981, to 27.7 in 1991, to 29.1 in 2000.[190] However, baby boomer women of the second generation not only have children later, but also have fewer children – see table 6.6. It is predicted that 'by the end of their reproductive span 21 per cent of second baby boomer women will remain childless'. This compares with 'only 13 per cent of first baby boom women'.[191]

The combination of these changes in partnership and family patterns have had very clear implications for the relationship between parents and children:

- Rising divorce and separation rates result in more single parenthood.

Table 6.6 Percentage of women remaining childless at selected ages by year of birth

Year of birth	Age 25	Age 35	Age 45
1925	46	19	17
1935	39	13	12
1945	34	11	9
1955	48	19	15
1965	60	25	–[a]
1975	65	–[a]	–[a]

[a] Figures not yet known
Source: Office for National Statistics, *Social Trends, England and Wales* 33, 2003

- Growing numbers of 'reconstituted families' involve children as well as stepchildren.
- Finally and potentially very important is the rise of the 'beanpole' family. As a result there will be smaller and more vertical family units, with fewer members in one generation but more generations coexisting and sharing care and household arrangements at the same time.[192]

Perhaps paradoxically, the overall impact of these changes will be to increase the level of interdependence between family members of generations. A simultaneous set of changes will see young parents apparently more likely to rely on grandparents to help juggle work and parenting commitments, while the growth of reconstituted families will increase the incidence of 'overlapping responsibilities' – parents and stepparents sharing responsibility for children from different partnerships and marriages – in the process helping to create more complex webs of mutual commitment, reciprocity and future dependence. When it comes to providing social care for older people, the set of considerations – financial, emotional and practical – involved in producing the best possible family arrangements, and their impact on patterns of financial inheritance and household structure, is far from straightforward.

Most welfare regimes were built on the assumption that the overwhelming majority of these activities would continue to take place within the private, informal setting of the family. In Britain today, for example, around two-thirds of the care provided to older people continues to come from within the family.[193] An expanding market for paid-for social care is probably a given, but the nature and flexibility of that market, and the extent to which it offers support options that can be mixed with the ongoing provision of informal family care, is a crucial factor.

The two forms of intergenerational flow we focus on here are caring – an intangible flow, which includes childcare and eldercare – and giving – a tangible flow, of which the most important aspect is the transfer of financial assets through inheritance. The reason for taking this rather economic focus is not because we think it is the most important aspect of family life – echoing an earlier Demos report, it may well be the least important.[194] The vast majority of care provided by families is based on the emotional bonds of love, not some rational economic analysis of the opportunity costs of providing it. But the economic perspective is important nonetheless. As Stein Ringen argues, the family performs a whole host of functions that would otherwise have to be undertaken by other, more visible parts of the economy: 'If the family becomes less efficient, we become more dependent on other arrangements and institutions for what families cannot manage.'[195]

Particularly because of the prevalence of divorce and separation among this generation, between 40 and 50 per cent of baby boomers are likely to be 'living solo' by the age of 75.[196] This is likely to have a significant impact on the demand for alternative sources of formal and informal care.[197] More than half of carers are looking after a parent.[198] But with fewer children to spread the load, and more parents living separately, the ageing baby boom generation will present a significant challenge to this arrangement. Though it may be partly offset by support from stepchildren and other overlapping commitments, in practical terms it is difficult to see how children will be able to support two separated parents as well as they could support two parents living together without making major sacrifices in other areas of their lives. At an emotional level, there is also some evidence to suggest that feelings of intergenerational obligation towards one or both of their parents may be altered by the experience of marital disruption.[199] With adults raising children later in their own lives, and growing time pressure on dual earner households, the availability of informal family care will be constrained.

Finally, the new interdependencies will have a big impact on financial inheritance. As we have seen, there is a partial trend towards greater involvement of grandparents in their grandchildren's lives, and the practice of 'inheritance skipping' will become more widespread. It has been estimated that £4 billion a year is already inherited by second generations.[200]

Whose needs, when?

All these changes point to greater uncertainty about who will need what, and when, during the cycle of family life. Grandparents could, and perhaps should, play a more significant role in helping young families meet the strains of child rearing in a long-hours culture, but it is increasingly likely that they will also depend on mutual support at specific and perhaps unpredictable times. Many baby boomers are likely to value their independence highly; though they are likely to want some involvement in family life (where they have children and grandchildren), the prospect of maintaining regular and demanding caring commitments may not be especially attractive.

Yet the children of baby boomers may not be able to expect the kind of steady growth in asset value that many of their parents have enjoyed up to now through stock market and house price increases. The triple demands of securing their own retirement provision, supporting parents when they come to need it and investing in the maintenance needs and future life chances of their children may hit these cohorts hard in decades to come, and in the process create a political backlash.

Such changes create a series of questions about how better support for families with caring responsibilities could be put in place. Public finances will benefit strongly from creating arrangements that allow families to create flexible forms of reciprocity, perhaps forging new forms of interdependence between three and four generations simultaneously, so that 'beanpole' families can work out more fluid combinations of caring and financial support, running in different directions at different times. For many older baby boomers there will be big questions to answer about how to manage the assets accumulated during a lifetime – the extent to which they can be spent in 'early old age' or eked out to provide greater security during a much longer period. Equally, the prospect of financial support, pension credits or underwriting of 'asset release' schemes, which enable extended families to invest more flexibly in specific needs at specific lifestages, could make a significant difference to the extent to which eldercare can be provided informally. For example, should grandparents receive tax or pension credits for taking on caring responsibilities? Should 'second generation' inheritance aimed at helping young people accumulate assets to be spent on education be encouraged through public policy? Or should inheritance tax be recalibrated to encourage intergenerational transfer through the state, which would have a more equalising effect on future opportunities for the young?

It seems that the answers to these questions should be generated not so much by trying to design separate policies targeted at different age groups, but by seeking to understand and then create supportive frameworks for arrangements in which creative combinations of caring activity, colocation, financial savings and subsidy can be put together to meet the differentiated needs of a widening range of extended family circumstances.

Towards a twenty-first-century welfare state?

These kind of solutions depend not just on brokering new forms of intergenerational solidarity within families, but on establishing clear principles of social justice and public expectation more widely. Over the next 30 years the biggest challenge to the welfare state will come from a *reappraisal of the structure of risk and need* at different points in the life stage. As a paper by Gosta Esping-Andersen has recently shown, the combination of demographic, labour market, social and technological change has combined to focus the long-term risks of disadvantage and poverty on children and adolescents in remarkably concentrated ways.[201] Where the postwar welfare consensus was built largely on the need to protect and insure those at risk of poverty and isolation in adult life, especially the elderly without adequate pensions or healthcare and those suffering adult unemployment, the burden of risk now falls more heavily on young people who for one reason or another are unable to build up the forms of financial, intellectual and cultural capital that improve their life chances as adults, through earning power, emotional resilience, social skills and cognitive development.

As a result, children who grow up in poverty, who do not get access to further educational opportunity and whose parenting and community support is diminished by other circumstances (including lack of time and attention from caring adults), are likely to remain disadvantaged and on the margins of society for the rest of their adult lives. Yet as Esping-Andersen shows, the pressure on working parents to work, earn and save while also providing the forms of intergenerational transfer that will benefit their children in the long run have become more extreme, especially in those countries that have moved rapidly towards higher female participation in the workforce without developing childcare infrastructure and subsidy on a similar scale.

If conflicts over public spending and political prioritisation of public resources loom, then this is probably the greatest and most difficult balancing act: how to develop more concentrated and proactive strategies for investing in children to help break the cycle of disadvantage and exclusion and create the conditions under which productive, fulfilling adult lives are possible for all, while simultaneously coping with the growing pressure for current spending to reflect the needs of a growing and vociferous older population.

Although it does not automatically provide the solution to this resource conflict, one measure that could help in its negotiation would be the introduction of *lifetime accounting*, through which individuals could accumulate investment, subsidy and other welfare transfers, receive subsidised loans for parenting breaks, higher education or lifelong learning, and combine with greater flexibility income from the various assets and entitlements that they might build up through a varied working life. Another possibility worthy of more detailed exploration is that government could support the creation of 'family trusts', in which these kinds of assets could be pooled and managed jointly by individual families, creating flexible vehicles for the negotiation of care and loan packages, and encouraging the transfer of resources towards the future needs of children, as well as those of older people.

In general terms, the introduction of intergenerational accounting principles into the management of national accounts would also aid transparent political debate about the costs and risks being borne by different generations at any one time. For example, if a nation discovers a source of unexpected wealth and income such as North Sea oil, other mineral extraction or the sale of common resources such as radio spectrum, should the revenues somehow be put 'in trust' for future generations? How do current patterns of environmental cost and risk distribution affect future needs and quality of life, as opposed to those of today? New forms of transparency and risk management in public investment could all help produce better long-term answers to this kind of question.

In the very long term, the right kinds of investment in children will have positive effects on the ability of younger generations to generate the wealth and the emotional resilience needed to support a high quality of life for older people. But in the meantime the transition between competing needs will have to be negotiated through politics. The extent to which the baby boomers can be convinced to trust politics and public policy to generate these positive outcomes will be crucial to the likelihood that the conflict can be negotiated by the whole of society, rather than by individuals and families seeking to defend their own interests and make their own private arrangements.

The birth of grey politics?

The rise of a 'grey politics' dominated by battles over pension rights, healthcare spending and community safety has long been predicted. So far, in the UK as in most industrialised countries, it has failed to materialise in any way that really changes mainstream public life. But the signs we have discovered and synthesised in this report give us confidence that members of the baby boomer generation will indeed carry their capacity for radicalism into old age, and in the process help to transform many of the institutions and expectations that hold society together.

British electoral politics is still dominated by competition for the middle ground. In practice this means capturing a constituency that has attained, or aspires towards, middle class comfort, has a sense of public decency, and wants the extremes of social disadvantage softened and opportunity widely distributed, together with a growing desire to shape and choose individual lifestyles and living arrangements. Over the next generation the centre of political gravity will inevitably shift towards a set of concerns that is not primarily anchored in the preoccupations of the prime-age working population with children to bring up, mortgages to pay off and careers to be developed.

If the baby boomers maintain their relatively high levels of nonconformism and stay politically engaged they will have a disproportionate impact on the way that political agendas are set. But there is no real indication so far of whether their activism, voting habits or party loyalties will help to hold British political culture in place or have a destabilising, fragmenting effect on the ways that parties compete for power and construct manifestos.

The likelihood is that grey politics will in fact be far more colourful than conventional wisdom has allowed. There is a huge opportunity for old and new political parties and pressure and advocacy groups to define agendas that will harness the latent power of an ageing population. In 2003 the Scottish Senior Citizens Unity Party was created led by John Swinburn, an enterprising independent MSP who sees the potential to create a new political force in a Scottish system that has been partly unravelled by the stagnation of traditional party politics, and that ironically may be furthest advanced within the UK towards a more pluralist, network-based approach to the construction of issue-based coalitions.

Several factors will influence the extent to which grey power affects electoral politics, from the willingness of senior citizens to vote and campaign to the geographical concentration of different age groups, from the ability of parties and campaigning organisations to develop new communication strategies to the opportunities for local office-holding and civic representation available to older people.

The baby boomer generation has the potential to rewrite the political agenda: around the distribution of traditional forms of public spending; around the new politics, focusing far more directly on 'quality of life' for individuals and communities; or with a generational clash of priorities around cultural values, cosmopolitanism and social equality. Far-sighted politicians and civic entrepreneurs should be turning their minds towards the issues that could act as mobilising flashpoints, with the potential to define political consciousness for a new generation. It may well be that issues that are currently treated as marginal could suddenly become central and emblematic, acting as the focal point for a much wider change. Such issues could range from the politics of life and death, especially euthanasia and the rationing of genetic therapies, to transport and public mobility, to access to green space and countryside, to participation in public culture and access to cultural resources, to discrimination in the workplace, to freedom of information and transparency in government decision-making. Pension rights, protection from financial shocks and access to health and social care will all be major concerns, but they will be negotiated in a changing cultural landscape, partly defined by whoever can generate the most imaginative political and organisational leadership.

This certainty suggests that more detailed investigation and debate of the underlying values carried forward by the baby boomers as they begin to define the 'new old' is worthwhile. In that context we conclude with 11 challenges that could form part of a positive agenda for all sectors, which could make society a better place to be old, and in turn increase the contribution that the 'new old' can make to the quality of everybody else's lives.

Challenge 1
Harness 'elderpreneurship' by creating new models of economic participation that allow older people to use their skills and assets creatively for longer.

Challenge 2
Remodel local life through the physical redesign of neighbourhoods and housing stock to maximise the integration and independence of older people in wider and more diverse communities.

Challenge 3
Create opportunities for civic participation and leadership that explicitly draw on the time and experience of older people, and widen the range of public representation. In the process, we need to re-create and validate a twenty-first-century notion of the 'community elder'.

Challenge 4
Build new forms of mutual and public support around the 'beanpole' family and redefine the rights and responsibilities of family life to maximise the value of intergenerational transfer in both directions, while making the needs of young children a central focus for all generations.

Challenge 5
Develop policies that not only prevent extreme pensioner poverty but also help prevent a significant minority of older people being pushed

into continued 'service-class' employment because of economic insecurity.

Challenge 6
Develop a sustainable market for social care that is intertwined with a robust, realistic emphasis on 'communities of care'.

Challenge 7
Capitalise on the baby boomers' insatiable appetite for learning by providing new forms of access and entitlement to knowledge and culture, and building new organisations capable of identifying, matching and refreshing labour market skills.

Challenge 8
Create workplace cultures that place as much emphasis on 'succession' and transfer of experience as they do on 'recruitment'.

Challenge 9
Develop a communications culture that is more effective at reaching, engaging and building trust by appealing to the growing desire to 'age well' and be treated as a mature consumer or citizen rather than catering to short-term appetites or targeting the assumption that the purpose of life is to perpetuate youth.

Challenge 10
Develop an approach to public service delivery that makes active participation in social networks and health-giving activities equal in status to the dispensation of standardised expert services.

Challenge 11
Stimulate a new public debate about the 'legacies' passed from one generation to another and the responsibilities of older generations towards the future.

An older society could be a wiser and a smarter society. We are in the midst of several long-term transformations of the basis on which everyday life is organised. But rarely does a society get the chance to prepare itself so far in advance and refresh its wider social values in the process. The next two decades will show whether we are up to the challenge.

Notes

1 E Burke, *Letter to a Member of the National Assembly, 1791* (Oxford: Woodstock, 1990).
2 Census 2001, www.statistics.gov.uk/census2001/press_release_uk/asp.
3 Office for National Statistics, *National Population Projections: 2000-based*, 2002.
4 J Chapman, *System Failure* (London: Demos, 2002); T Bentley, 'Letting go: complexity, individualism and the Left', *Renewal* 10, no 1 (Winter 2002); P Skidmore, *Beyond Measure* (London: Demos, 2003).
5 Government green paper, *Simplicity, Security and Choice: Working and saving for retirement*, December 2002, www.dwp.gov.uk/consultations/consult/2002/pensions/gp.pdf.
6 Figures taken from United Nations Department of Economic and Social Affairs, Population Division, *World Population Ageing, 1950–2050* (New York: United Nations, 2002).
7 ONS, *National Population projections, 2000-based.*
8 Census 2001, www.statistics.gov.uk/census2001/press_release_uk/ asp.
9 ONS, *National Population projections, 2000-based.*
10 UNDESA, Population Division, *World Population Ageing, 1950–2050.*
11 ONS, *National population projections, 2000-based.*
12 World Bank, *Averting the Old Age Crisis: Policies to protect the old and promote growth* (New York: Oxford University Press, 1994).
13 Government green paper, *Simplicity, Security and Choice.*
14 Ibid.
15 See, for example, P Collinson, 'Stakeholder pensions flop', *Guardian*, 23 November 2002.
16 Consumers' Association, *Blueprint for a National Pensions Policy* (London: Consumers' Association, 2003).
17 Government green paper, *Simplicity, Security and Choice.*
18 By way of an international comparison, the average retirement age is even lower in much of continental Europe (age 60.3 in Germany, age 58.8 in Italy,

age 60.4 in the Netherlands). It is slightly higher in Sweden (age 63.7) and the United States (age 64.6) and considerably higher in Japan (age 68.5). See OECD, *Ageing and Income.*

19 Government green paper, *Simplicity, Security and Choice.*
20 Ibid.
21 Ibid.
22 PIU, *Winning the Generation Game* (London: Performance and Innovation Unit, 2000).
23 Government green paper, *Simplicity, Security and Choice.*
24 Ibid.
25 European Directive on Equal Treatment in Employment and Occupation, Nov 2000; for more details see www.britishcouncil.org/diversity/text/age_legislationtx.htm and http://europa.eu.int/scadplus/leg/en/cha/c10823.htm.
26 See www.agepositive.gov.uk/champions.cfm?sectionid=87.
27 Department for Trade and Industry, *Equality and Diversity: Age matters, age consultation 2003*, www.dti.gov.uk/er/equality/age_consultation.pdf.
28 D Wanless, *Securing our Future Health: Taking a long-term view*, 2002, www.hm-treasury.gov.uk/Consultations_and_Legislation/wanless/consult_wanless_final.cfm.
29 D Metz, 'The politics of population ageing', *Political Quarterly*, July–Sept, 2002.
30 Ibid.
31 Wanless, *Securing our Future Health.*
32 HM Treasury, *The Strength to Make Long-term Decisions: Investing in an enterprising, fairer Britain*, Economic and Fiscal Strategy Report and Financial Statement and Budget Report April 2002 (London: The Stationery Office, 2002).
33 See www.doh.gov.uk/nsf/olderpeopleexecfore.htm.
34 Royal Commission on Long Term Care for the Elderly, *With Respect to Old Age: Long term care – rights and responsibilities,* 1999, Cm 4192, www.archive.official-documents.co.uk/document/cm41/4192/4192-02.htm#4.
35 See www.doh.gov.uk/govresp.htm.
36 See www.doh.gov.uk/nsf/olderpeopleexecstand8.htm.
37 'Thousand of places lost in crisis-hit care homes', *Guardian*, 18 July 2002.
38 The study concluded that the fees currently paid by local councils are between £75 and £85 a week below the reasonable cost of running an efficient and good-quality care home. See www.jrf.org.uk/pressroom/releases/190602.asp.
39 J Carvel, 'Milburn retreats on care home standards', *Guardian*, 20 August 2002.
40 K Dunnell and D Dix, 'Are we looking forward to a longer and healthier retirement?' *Health Statistics Quarterly* 6, quoted in Wanless, *Securing our Future Health.*
41 NHS *R&D Strategic Review*, 'Ageing and Age-Associated Disease and Disability' (1999) quoted in Metz, 'The politics of population ageing'.
42 Wanless, *Securing our Future Health.*

43 ONS, *National Population Projections, 2000-based*; Government Actuary's Department, 2003; General Register Office for Scotland, *Scotland Census*, 2001, 2003; Northern Ireland Statistics and Research Agency, 2003.
44 Census 2001, www.statistics.gov.uk/census2001/pop2001/united_kingdom_ages.asp.
45 The Future Foundation & nVision, *Changing Lives* (The Future Foundation/Taylor Nelson Sofres, 2002).
46 MORI, Social Values, 1999. See below for discussion of the distinction between early and late baby boomers.
47 MORI, Social Values, 1999.
48 MORI, Trust in Public Institutions, 2003.
49 MORI, Social Values, 2002.
50 Defined as the highest median individual gross income among different age groups. See Office for National Statistics, *Family Resources Survey, Great Britain 1999–2000.*
51 ONS, *Family Resources Survey, Great Britain 1999–2000*. This may become more significant once new and more effective financial products for unlocking equity from home ownership become available. See A Dilnot 'Don't panic, pensions are not in crisis', *Guardian*, 3 Oct 2002.
52 MORI, Social Values, 2002.
53 MORI, Social Values, 1999.
54 MORI, Social Values, 1999.
55 J Curtis, 'Grey hair, wrinkles and money to burn', *Financial Times*, 8 Oct 2002.
56 See MJ Weiss, 'Chasing Youth', *American Demographics*, Oct 2002.
57 Cf. S Chen, 'Citizenship, consumerism and the public realm', *Renewal* 11, no 2 (2003); J LeGrand, 'The least worse way to improve public services: the case for competition', *Renewal* 11, no 2 (2003).
58 eg D Osborne and T Gaebler, *Reinventing Government: How the entrepreneurial spirit is transforming the public sector* (London: Penguin, 1993).
59 Prime Minister's Office of Public Services Reform, *Reforming Our Public Services: Principles into practice* (London: Office of Public Services Reform, 2002).
60 MORI, Trust in Public Institutions, 2003.
61 MORI, Corporate Social Responsibility, 2002.
62 T Bentley, 'Letting go'.
63 R Jowell, 'Do people's attitudes change as they age?', David Hobman ACIOG Annual Lecture, January 2002.
64 A Barlow et al, 'Just a piece of paper? Marriage and cohabitation', in NatCen's, *British Social Attitudes Survey*, 18th Report (London: Sage Publications, 2001).
65 Barlow et al, 'Just a Piece of Paper?'.
66 Jowell 'Do people's attitudes change as they age?'
67 L Clarke and K Thomson, 'Teenage mums', in NatCen's, *British Social Attitudes Survey*, 18th Report (London: Sage Publications, 2001).
68 MORI, Social Values, 1999.
69 MORI, Political Concerns, 2002.

70 A Gould and N Stratford, 'Illegal drugs: high and lows', in NatCen's, *British Social Attitudes Survey*, 19th Report (London: Sage Publications, 2002).
71 MORI, Social Values, 1999.
72 MORI, European Public Opinion and Foreign Policy, 2002.
73 Ibid.
74 M Evandrou and J Falkingham, 'Looking back to look forward: Lessons from four birth cohorts for ageing in the 21st century', *Population Trends* 99 (Spring 2000). See also M Evandrou 'Social care: today and beyond 2020', in M Evandrou (ed), *Baby Boomers – Ageing in the 21st Century* (London: Age Concern, 1997).
75 MORI, Trust in Public Institutions, 2003.
76 MORI, Social Values, 1999.
77 Evandrou (ed), *Baby Boomers – Ageing in the 21st Century*.
78 Ibid.
79 82% of early baby boomers say that they like to feel that they are in touch with what is happening in other countries in the world; only 73% of the late baby boomers feel the same. 39% of early baby boomers feel that they are more a citizen of the world than of their country; only 31% of the second generation baby boomers agree. On the MORI Social Values indices the late baby boomer generation is much less correlated with 'global village' (meaning a 'feeling of being a citizen of the world and desiring to have experience of and contact with other countries') than the older baby boomers. MORI, Social Values, 1999.
80 Whereas 35% of younger baby boomers believe that 'it is a good thing that foreigners in Britain keep the lifestyle which they had at home', only 27.5% of the older baby boomers agree. Again the MORI Social Values indices confirm this attitudinal difference, as late baby boomers correlated much stronger with 'multiculturalism' (meaning 'respect for and interest in the other cultures existing in British society founded upon a goal of cultural enrichment') than the earlier generation of baby boomers. According to the *British Social Attitudes Survey* 21% of second generation baby boomers have 'any racial prejudice' compared with 24% of first generation baby boomers. MORI, Social Values, 2002; G Evans, 'In search of tolerance', in NatCen's, *British Social Attitudes Survey*, 19th Report (London: Sage Publications, 2002).
81 Only 15% of young baby boomers have traditional views of marriage compared with 23% of the older baby boomers. Whereas 40% of second generation baby boomers think that 'Homosexual sex is not wrong at all' only 32% of first generation baby boomers agree. Jowell, 'Do people's attitudes change as they age?'; Barlow et al, 'Just a Piece of Paper'; Evans, 'In search of tolerance'.
82 ONS, *New Earnings Survey*, 2001.
83 Ibid.
84 ONS, *Family Resources Survey, Great Britain 1999–2000*.

85 Government green paper, *Simplicity, Security and Choice*. Age group here classified as 35–59.
86 ONS, *Social Trends* 32, 2002.
87 ONS, *Health Statistics Quarterly* 15 (Autumn 2002).
88 Women and Equality Unit, *Key Indicators of Women's Position in Britain* (London: DTI, 2002).
89 ONS, *Social Trends* 32, 2002.
90 Calculations are based on figures in ONS, *Labour Force Survey*, 2000. Approximations are a result of using a slightly different age group (35–59).
91 A version of this argument has been put forward by Polly Toynbee ('Looking for an enemy', *Guardian*, 14 Oct 2000).
92 Jowell, 'Do people's attitudes change as they age?'
93 Ibid.
94 Ibid.
95 C Bromley and J Curtice, 'Where have all the voters gone?', in NatCen's, *British Social Attitudes Survey*, 19th Report (London: Sage Publications, 2002).
96 Jowell, 'Do people's attitudes change as they age?'
97 eg R Inglehart, 'From class-based to value-based politics' in P Mair (ed) *The West European Party System* (Oxford: Oxford University Press, 1990).
98 ONS, *Family Resources Survey, Great Britain 1999–2000.*
99 MORI Social Values, 2002.
100 MORI Social Values, 1999.
101 Ibid.
102 Government green paper, *Simplicity, Security and Choice.*
103 Foresight Ageing Population Panel, *The Age Shift – Priorities for Action* (London: Department for Trade and Industry, December 2000).
104 Evandrou, 'Social care: today and beyond 2020'.
105 H Wilkinson, *Crèche Barriers* (London: Demos, 2002).
106 L Kellaway, 'Rise of the supergran', *Financial Times*, 2 May 2003.
107 G Dench and J Ogg, *Grandparenting in Britain – A Baseline Study* (London: Institute of Community Studies, 2002). See also Wilkinson, *Crèche Barriers.*
108 J Banks et al, *Retirement, Pensions and the Adequacy of Saving: A guide to the debate* (London: The Institute for Fiscal Studies, Sept 2002).
109 This is compared with 41% of 15- to 34-year-olds and 39% of those aged over 55 to have this preference. MORI, Social Values, 1999.
110 For a brief overview of these categories, see PIU, *Social Capital: a discussion paper* (London: Performance and Innovation Unit, 2002).
111 In this sense, we are building on earlier Demos work, which sought to apply the concept of entrepreneurship to non-commercial contexts. See C Leadbeater, *The Rise of the Social Entrepreneur* (London: Demos, 1997); C Leadbeater and S Goss, *Civic Entrepreneurship* (London: Demos, 1998).
112 Social Investment Task Force, *Enterprising Communities: Wealth beyond welfare* (2000), www.enterprising-communities.org.uk.
113 See www.bridgesventures.com.
114 See www.cdfa.org.uk/.
115 L Howland, L Humphrey and C

Tims, *Community into Business* (London: Demos, 2003).

116 See www.dti.gov.uk/cics/index.htm.

117 See www.princes-trust.org.uk/.

118 See www.sbs.gov.uk/content/docs/SFLG_booklet.pdf.

119 For an overview, see OECD, *Measuring What People Know: Human capital accounting for the knowledge economy* (Paris: Organisation for Economic Co-operation and Development, 1996).

120 European Directive on Equal Treatment in Employment and Occupation, Nov 2000.

121 A Dilnot, 'Don't panic, pensions are not in crisis', *Guardian*, 4 Oct 2002.

122 Figures from Norwich Union Equity Release, 2003.

123 Kawachi et al in PIU, *Social Capital.*

124 PIU, *Social Capital.*

125 PIU, *Social Capital.*

126 PIU, *Winning the Generation Game.*

127 Experience Corps was inspired by and to some extent modelled on a number of American not-for-profit organisations. These include a US Experience Corps (focused on schools), SeniorCorps and Civic Ventures, another not-for-profit body founded to extend the work of the Experience Corps. Its aim is 'to expand the contribution of older Americans to society and to help transform the ageing of America into a source of individual and social renewal'. For more information see www.experiencecorps.co.uk and www.civicventures.org.

128 Berkman and Glass, in PIU, *Social Capital.*

129 Evandrou and Falkingham, 'Looking back to look forward'. See also Evandrou, 'Social care'.

130 G Brown and T Harris, *Social Origins of Depression* (Tavistock: 1998), quoted in PIU, *Social Capital.*

131 MORI, Social Values, 1999.

132 MORI, Social Values, 1999.

133 Given a base of 100 baby boomers score 96, whereas those aged 55 and over score 158. MORI, Social Values, 1999.

134 Where the base is 100 the early boomers score 93, the late boomers 121 and those aged 55 and over just 33. MORI, Social Values, 1999.

135 MORI, Social Values, 2002.

136 ONS, *Social Trends* 32, 2002.

137 G C Wenger, 'Nurturing networks', *The Wealth and Poverty of Networks,* Demos Collection Issue 12 (London: Demos, 1997).

138 C Alexander, *A Pattern Language* (New York: Oxford University Press, 1977).

139 Ibid.

140 For more information see www.homezones.org.

141 J Wilsdon and D Stedman Jones, *The Politics of Bandwidth* (London: Demos, 2002).

142 G Thomas and G Hocking, *Other People's Children* (London: Demos 2003).

143 See www.bbbsa.org.

144 See www.bbbsi.org.

145 D Prescott, 'What a difference a day makes – involving businesses in day care', Kings College Lecture, 2002

146 See www.aarp.org/connections/mar2002/fitness.html.
147 MORI, *Nestle Family Monitor – Lifelong Learning and Volunteering*, 2000.
148 It has been suggested that older generations traditionally lack confidence in their ability to 'keep up' with younger learners. J Smith and A Spurling, *Lifelong Learning: Riding the tiger* (London: Cassell, 1999).
149 e-MORI Technology Tracker, August 2002.
150 T Bentley, *It's Democracy, Stupid* (London: Demos, 2001).
151 See www.benefitscheckup.org/.
152 See www.aarp.org/.
153 See www.elderhostel.org/welcome/home.asp.
154 See www.learningannex.com.
155 A Dyson, A Millward and E Todd, *A Study of the Extended Schools Demonstration Projects* Research Report RR381 (Newcastle: SNRC/DfES, undated).
156 Ibid.
157 See www.communiversity.org.uk; www.can-online.org.uk.
158 Comedia/Demos, *Park Life: Urban parks and social renewal* (London: Demos, 1995).
159 Ibid.
160 Ibid.
161 ONS, *Labour Force Survey*, 2000.
162 Royal Commission on Long Term Care for the Elderly, *With Respect to Old Age: Rights and responsibilities*, 1999, www.archive.official-documents.co.uk/document/ cm41/4192/4192-08.htm#88.
163 'Chapter 9 – Black and Minority Ethnic Elderly: Perspectives on Long-Term Care', Royal Commission on Long Term Care for the Elderly, *With Respect to Old Age*, Volume 1, Part 1 – *The Context of Long-Term Care Policy*, 1999, www.archive.official-documents.co.uk/document/cm41/4192/v1ch9.pdf.
164 T Bentley, H McCarthy and M Mean, *Inside Out: Rethinking inclusive communities* (London, Demos: 2003).
165 See www.aarp.org/, www.segundajuventud.org/spanish/.
166 MORI, Social Values, 1999.
167 MORI, Social Values, 1999.
168 I Christie and L Jarvis, 'How green are your values?', in NatCen's, *British Social Attitudes Survey*, 18th Report (London: Sage Publications, 2001).
169 MORI, *Corporate Social Responsibility*, 2002.
170 This is in line with long-run attitudinal trends. See Jowell, 'Do people's attitudes change as they age?'
171 MORI Estimates.
172 MORI, *Trust in Public Institutions*, 2003.
173 A Walker, 'Political participation and representation of older people in Europe' in A Walker and G Naegele (ed), *The politics of Old Age in Europe* (Buckingham: Open University Press, 1999).
174 e-MORI Technology Tracker, May 2003.
175 MORI, Social Values, 1999.
176 See www.aarp.org/community/ and www.bbb.org.uk.
177 National Insurance Fund, *Long Term Financial Estimates*, Quinquennial Review, Cm 4406 (2002).
178 Ibid.

179 Ibid. Assumes the basic state pension continues to be uprated in line with prices.
180 *A New Contract for Welfare: Partnership in pensions*, presented to Parliament by the Secretary of State for Social Security, Cm 4179, December 1998.
181 Ibid.
182 Figures from consumer research conducted by Norwich Union Equity Release, 2003. Here 'children' are defined as aged 30 or over, whose parents are aged over 50 and own a home worth at least £50,000.
183 Evandrou and Falkingham, 'Looking back to look forward'.
184 Evandrou and Falkingham, 'Looking back to look forward'.
185 ONS, *Social Trends* 33, 2003.
186 Evandrou and Falkingham, 'Looking back to look forward'.
187 ONS, *Marriage, Divorce and Adoption Statistics, England and Wales* 2000.
188 Falkingham, 'Who are the baby boomers?'.
189 Falkingham, 'Who are the baby boomers?'.
190 ONS, *Social Trends* 33, 2003.
191 Falkingham, 'Who are the baby boomers?'.
192 Dench and Ogg, *Grandparenting in Britain*.
193 F McGlone and N Cronin, *A Crisis in Care?* (London: Family Policy Studies Centre, 1994).
194 S Ringen, *The Family in Question* (London: Demos, 1998).
195 Ibid.
196 Evandrou and Falkingham, 'Looking back to look forward'.
197 'The cost of long-term care now and in the future' in Royal Commission on Long Term Care for the Elderly, *With Respect to Old Age*, Volume 1, Part 1 – *The Context of Long-Term Care Policy*, 1999, www.archive.official-documents.co.uk/document/cm41/4192/v1ch1.pdf.
198 J Maher and H Green, *Carers 2000* (London: Office for National Statistics, 2002).
199 Evandrou and Falkingham, 'Looking back to look forward'.
200 ILC-UK/Future Foundation, *The Giving Age – Inheritance in the Context of an Ageing Population*, 2002.
201 G Esping-Andersen, *Investing in Children: Towards a new welfare equilibrium*. Working Paper for the New Welfare State Working Group of the Progressive Governance Summit, 11–13 July 2003.